W9-AMP-052

Basic
Library
Skills

Basic Library Skills

Third Edition

by
Carolyn Wolf
and Richard Wolf

McFarland & Company, Inc., Publishers
Jefferson, North Carolina, and London

British Library Cataloguing-in-Publication data are available

Library of Congress Cataloguing-in-Publication Data

Wolf, Carolyn E., 1941–
    Basic library skills / by Carolyn Wolf and Richard Wolf. – 3rd
ed.
    p. cm.
    Includes bibliographical references and index.
    ISBN 0-89950-895-2 (sewn softcover : 50# alk. paper) ∞
    1. Libraries—United States.   2. Searching, Bibliographical.
I. Wolf, Richard, 1938– . II. Title.
Z710.W64   1993 c- 1
025.56—dc20   92-51100
                                                      CIP

Manufactured in the United States of America

McFarland & Company, Inc., Publishers
  Box 6ll, Jefferson, North Carolina 28640

Preface and Acknowledgments

This text is designed to be a self-contained short course in the use of the library, not an exhaustive treatment of the subject. The intent is to provide a quick and easy way to learn to do library research. One could use it as an adjunct to a course in library usage or as part of an introductory English composition course. Also, it might serve as a self-paced instructional sequence for all students. Students have used the first two editions of this book as the major text in a college course in library usage. An author used the text in a graduate course in research methods. These courses included 15 hours of classroom instruction. The student should master basic library skills in about 25 to 30 hours. This will vary according to the intellectual skills of the student and his or her study technique. Furthermore, the self-paced design of the text allows students to learn the material at individual speeds.

The authors included only material that was considered essential for mastery of basic library skills. One cannot learn to use the library by working through the text only. Mastery demands "hands on" experience and practice in the library. The concepts in the text are generalizable to all libraries. Materials that were deemed to be too specific were omitted.

The authors determined which skills were needed by library users. Each chapter lists the performance skills, called *objectives*. These statements tell the student what is to be learned in the chapter. After studying the materials in each chapter the student should be able to perform the objectives. These objectives are practical and have immediate application for the student. The authors omitted theoretical or abstract materials that were unrelated to specific tasks.

Learning psychologists have discovered that students learn more efficiently if they are presented with and attend to stated objectives. Therefore, it is recommended that students attend to the objectives before studying each chapter.

The *exercises* give students hands-on experience by applying rules stated in the text to situations that approach real "research problems." Students also will find the *new or unusual terms* found in the text listed at the back of the chapter. They should be able to define these after studying the text. Bibliographies of examples used in the text and other resources are also included after each chapter.

Finally, the library is the essence of the educational institution. It is unfortunate that some students have negative feelings toward the library. These feelings will become more positive as students learn to use the library. That is the goal of this text.

The authors would like to thank the H. W. Wilson Company, Marquis Who's Who, Inc., Oryx Press, American Library Association and the American Psychological Association for permission to use examples of their publications:

Figure 5.1 *Cumulative Book Index*, May 1991, page 171 (v. 94, no. 5). Copyright © 1991 by the H. W. Wilson Company. Material reproduced with permission of the publisher.

Figure 5.2 *Bibliographic Index*, April 1991, page 100. Copyright © 1991 by the H. W. Wilson Company. Material reproduced with permission of the publisher.

Figure 6.1 *Book Review Index, 1990 Cumulation*, Neil E. Walker and Beverly Baer, editors. Copyright © 1991 by Gale Research Inc. Reproduced by permission of the publisher.

Figure 6.2 *Book Review Digest*, May 1991, page 210. Copyright © 1991 by the H. W. Wilson Company. Material reproduced with permission of the publisher.

Figure 8.1 *General Science Index*, May 1991, page 343 (v. 13, no. 10). Copyright © by the H. W. Wilson Company. Material reproduced with permission of the publisher.

Figure 8.2 *Psychological Abstracts* reprinted with permission of the American Psychological Association, publisher of *Psychological Abstracts* and the PsycINFO Database (copyright 1967–1991 by the American Psychological Association).

Figure 8.5 *New Serials Titles*, February 1991, page 97. Reprinted with permission of the American Library Association.

Figure 9.1 *Thesaurus of Psychological Index Terms* reprinted with permission of the American Psychological Association, publisher of *Psychological Abstracts* and the PsycINFO Database (copyright 1967–1991 by the American Psychological Association).

Figure 10.1 *Short Story Index*, 1989, page 84. Copyright © 1989 by the

H. W. Wilson Company. Material reproduced with permission of the publisher.

Figure 10.2 *Essay and General Literature*, 1990, page 145. Copyright © 1990 by the H. W. Wilson Company. Material reproduced with permission of the publisher.

Figure 10.3 *Fiction Catalog*, 12th edition, page 373. Copyright © 1991 by the H. W. Wilson Company. Material reproduced with permission of the publisher.

Figure 11.4 *Thesaurus of ERIC Descriptors*, 12th ed., copyright 1990 by the Oryx Press, 4041 N. Central at Indian School Rd., Phoenix, AZ 85012. Used by permission of the Oryx Press.

Figure 12.1 *Biography Index*, May 1991 (v. 45, no. 3). Copyright © 1991 by the H. W. Wilson Company. Material reproduced with permission of the publisher.

Figure 12.2 *Who's Who in America*, 1990–1991 edition, vol. 2. Copyright © 1990–91, Marquis Who's Who, Inc. Reprinted by permission.

Figure 12.3 *Contemporary Authors*, Volume 131, edited by Susan M. Trosky. Copyright © 1991 by Gale Research Inc. Reproduced by permission of the publisher.

Additional thanks goes to Bruce Endries for supplying the cover photo.

Table of Contents

Introduction: A Brief
Historical Perspective

The earliest books, especially those written on papyrus, were scrolls. Users stored them in earthen jars to protect them from water, insects and fire. Early civilizations, such as the Egyptians, had libraries and librarians to store these scrolls. The library at Alexandria, Egypt, was one of the largest of the ancient libraries and contained more than 700,000 scrolls. Julius Caesar destroyed most of the library in 47 B.C., and the Christians further damaged it in A.D. 391. Ancient books contain references to the library, part of which still stands, and one may find book titles and the names of some librarians on the walls.

Discoverers have found other ancient libraries. The Library of Assurbanipal at Nineveh, dated at 668–626 B.C., contained about 25,000 clay tablets. Archaeologists have recovered many of these tablets, and about 21,000 of them, whole or fragmentary, are in the British Museum. Many other ancient libraries were destroyed by war and invading barbarians.

During the Dark or Middle Ages, the monastic libraries preserved much of the classical literature and knowledge. The monks copied books in the scriptorium, a writing room–library combination. Many books were not only copied but translated from Greek and other languages. Early medieval universities were located near monasteries that had libraries. Students waited long periods of time and paid large sums of money to scribes who copied books for them.

The invention of printing by movable type is generally credited to Johannes Gutenberg of Mainz, Germany, sometime between 1450 and

1455. Scholars believe that Gutenberg printed the first complete book, a Bible in 1456. The art of printing spread rapidly across Europe and arrived in the New World in 1539. With the spread of the technology of printing came uses other than the reproduction of Bibles, psalters and other religious books. Broadsheets, pamphlets, newssheets and other forms of spreading information and news were developed. American colonists printed the first book in 1639.

During the mid–18th century came the formation of national libraries. The British Museum, a library and museum, was founded in 1733. The nucleus of the library was the personal collections of Sir Robert Cotton, Robert Harley, Earl of Oxford, and Sir Hans Sloan. The holdings were enlarged in 1757 with the addition of the Royal Library, books collected by the kings from Edward IV to George II. The United States Congress founded the Library of Congress in 1800 as a research library. The British burned the library in 1814 during the attack on Washington. The collection was rebuilt around the personal library of Thomas Jefferson, who was also instrumental in convincing other book collectors to send their personal collections to the library.

Copyright offices have been established in national libraries for developing the national libraries and insuring the completeness of its collection (at a somewhat small cost to the government).

The first public library in the United States was founded in 1833 in Peterborough, New Hampshire. The first major public library was established in Boston in 1852 but was not opened until 1854. In the 1900s, Andrew Carnegie began donating money to communities throughout the country for the construction of libraries. These libraries were to be open to the public free of charge. Often Carnegie built libraries in small rural communities that would have been unable to build their libraries without this financial assistance. Many of these libraries are still in use today.

In 1969 the term "media center" came into general use for the school library. Most of today's institutional libraries are truly media centers, offering nonprint resources (such as audio and video recordings) besides traditional printed material. Many libraries today also participate in networks, groups of libraries cooperating to share their resources. With the high costs and diversity of materials it is necessary to share resources. Such sharing enables libraries to fulfill their mission; to serve as repositories of recorded history and culture, making information readily available for the individual.

Suggested Readings

Cater, John, ed. *Printing and the Mind of Man: A Descriptive Catalogue Illustrating the Impact of Print on the Evolution of Western Civilization During Five Centuries.* New York: Holt, Rinehart and Winston, 1967.

Christ, Karl. *The Handbook of Medieval Library History.* Metuchen, NJ: Scarecrow, 1984.

Diringer, David. *The Book Before Printing: Ancient, Medieval and Oriental.* New York: Dover, 1982 (reprint of 1953 ed.).

Dunkin, Paul Shaner. *Tales of Melvil's Mouser; Or Much Ado About Libraries.* New York: R. R. Bowker, 1970.

Goodrum, Charles A. *The Library of Congress.* New York: Praeger, 1974.

_____. *Treasures of the Library of Congress.* New York: H. N. Abrams, 1980.

Hobson, Anthony Robert Alwyn. *Great Libraries.* London: Weidenfeld & Nicholson, 1970.

Jackson, Donald. *The Story of Writing.* New York: Taplinger, 1981.

Keep, Austin Baxter. *The Library in Colonial America.* New York: B. Franklin, 1970.

McMurtrie, Douglas C. *The Book: The Story of Printing and Bookmaking.* New York: Covici, Friede, 1937.

New York Public Library. *Censorship: 500 Years of Conflict.* New York: Oxford University Press, 1984.

Oswald, John Clyde. *Benjamin Franklin, Printer.* Detroit: Gale Research Co., 1974.

Rosenberry, Cecil R. *For the Government and People of This State: A History of the New York State Library.* Albany: University of the State of New York, 1970.

Winkler, Paul A. *Reader in the History of Books and Printing.* Englewood, CO: Information Handling Services, 1978.

1. A Walking Tour of the Library

Objectives

After studying this chapter the student shall be able to
  • locate the various facilities of the library in a quick and efficient manner
  • draw a map indicating where these facilities are
  • identify relevant staff members and the services each provide
  • find the location of each staff member and show this on the map
  • list the hours the library is open and when its constituent services are available
  • state the policies of the library in terms of borrowing regulations, open and closed stacks, overdue fines, and the general regulations regarding the use of the building

General Information

The aim of this chapter is to help the student identify and locate basic services offered by the library. To use the library extensively, the student should familiarize himself with its layout, facilities, resources and staff. To do this, a walking tour is essential. Many libraries give official tours by staff members. If these are not available, then the student should take his own tour.

As the student walks through the library he or she should note where all services and materials are located. For future reference a map or schematic diagram is helpful. Since each library is unique, the

5

location of these components will vary greatly. The student should therefore diagram the library that they will use. Some libraries provide maps. These may be very specific or somewhat incomplete. In the latter case, additional information may be added.

The next stop on the walking tour is the circulation desk, since it is the "hub" where most of the business of the library is conducted. The main function of the circulation desk is to keep books moving in and out of the library. Students should familiarize themselves with the rules for book circulation (length of loan period, identification required when checking out books) and the policy for fines and lost books.

Libraries usually have a special system for reserve materials, which may include books, journal articles, tapes and other sources that are set aside for use by students in their courses. There may be special restrictions on the use of these materials. If this reserve area is not located near the circulation desk, a point should be made to find it.

A critical area of the library is the reference section. The reference librarian's main function is to provide help in using the reference materials provided by the library. This person can locate sources to be consulted to answer specific questions. The reference desk is usually located near the entrance or the circulation desk.

On the next stop of the walking tour, the student should locate the card catalog. Nearly everything the library has is listed here. (The use of the card catalog is explained in Chapter 2.) The catalog is usually located near the reference desk. Some libraries have given up the card catalog and are using computer terminals (On-line Public Access Catalog—OPACS *see* Chapter 3) and microfiche cards. If the library has "closed" and removed its card catalog, then find the computer terminals or microfiche copy (COM) of the catalog. A "closed" catalog means that no cards have been added after the "closed" date and the student must consult the OPACs or COM catalog for recent additions to the library's collection.

A brief walk through the bookshelves (stacks) will enable the user to get a general overview of how the books are grouped. Notice should be taken of the numbering system and how it relates to the catalog. Since the use of the catalog is thoroughly explained in chapters 2 and 3, just a brief overview is necessary during the tour. The student could randomly select a book from the catalog to see if it can be located on

Opposite: **Finding a sunny, quiet place to read or study after your walking tour.**

the shelves. Special sections, such as fiction, new books and rare books, should be located and added to the map.

Most libraries have a separate area or special reading room for periodicals, magazines and journals. There is usually a periodical's desk or office, which may be staffed by a librarian or student assistants to aid in locating or identifying specific items. Most libraries do not permit the free circulation of periodicals since they have heavy use for short periods of time. The rules for the use of the periodical sections should be studied as they vary between libraries. Some libraries keep back files of newspapers or microfilms of them. The student should locate where these are kept and find out how to use the microfilm readers.

A recently burgeoning part of library services is "nonprint" (or "non-book") materials. These materials include microprint formats (microfilm, microfiche), audio and video tapes, records, slides and 16mm and 33mm films. Unfortunately, these materials may be underused because students think they are difficult to use. Students should familiarize themselves with all the materials that are available and with how to operate the equipment. A valuable use of time might be just looking at an example from these specific materials and operating the equipment. The location of the materials and the equipment should be noted on the library map.

An important adjunct of the library is the copying service. One should find where services are, how to use them with the various types of materials, and any charges connected with their use. If the machines are coin operated, change should be brought to the library, as some librarians find it distracting and time-consuming to make change. There may be special copying areas in the library. These should be located and indicated on the map. The prudent use of copying is suggested, and copyright laws should be followed. The student should not make multiple copies of copyrighted materials without permission of the publisher since it is illegal to do so.

The location of certain items that may not appear essential can make the use of the library a more pleasant and efficient experience. Such items include stairs and elevators, lavatories, water fountains, pencil sharpeners, paper cutters and telephones. These should be shown on the map. The student should also include the location of listening rooms for records and tapes and special areas for typewriters, computers and calculators.

The student should become familiar with the staff of the library. They are there for the user's benefit and are usually eager to help. It is important to remember that the library aides are employed to help find information and expect to be called upon. To the librarian there is no such thing as a "stupid question."

Libraries generally divide their staff into two major departments, public services and technical services. The public services employees are "up front" and interact with the library patrons or visitors. They work at the circulation, reference, reserve and periodical desks. Knowing the names of the people who work in the public services areas may be useful. The technical services employees are the "behind-the-scenes" staff. They are usually divided into two departments, cataloging and acquisitions. The acquisitions staff is responsible for purchasing books, periodicals, nonprint and other materials and may be consulted if students wish the library to purchase materials on an individual basis. The cataloging staff is responsible for adding new acquisitions to the catalog and making resources ready for the shelves and circulation. Finally, the head librarian supervises all staff and is available to solve problems that cannot be handled by the staff. The name and location of the head librarian's office should be noted.

The rules, regulations and policies of the library are instituted and maintained for the benefit of the users. A copy of the library manual should be obtained and some of these questions should be answered by referring to the manual: What services are available at what hours? What are the borrowing regulations? What are the rules for the reserve materials? What are the fines for overdue books? What is the policy on lost books? Does the library permit smoking, eating or drinking and where are these things permitted? What are the security precautions? (Knowing these may avoid embarrassment when leaving the library.)

After the tour the student should complete a map containing the following locations:

1. circulation desk	11. copying machines
2. reference desk	12. head librarian's office
3. reserve desk	13. cataloging department
4. reference section	14. acquisitions department
5. periodicals section	15. card catalog (or OPAC)
6. reading room	16. special collections
7. book stacks	17. rare book room
8. newspapers	18. lavatories
9. microfilm section	19. water fountains
10. readers	20. pencil sharpener(s)

21. stairs and elevators
22. exits
23. smoking areas
24. computers for public use
25. computer software
26. atlases
27. public telephones

A list of the people who work in the library should contain at least the names of the following:

1. head librarian
2. circulation department head
3. reference department head
4. periodicals department head
5. cataloging department head
6. acquisitions department head

Exercises for Chapter 1

1. Complete a map locating the facilities listed earlier.
2. List the name(s) of the person(s) responsible for various library services.
3. Complete the following chart of library hours:

	Library Opens	Library Closes
Sunday		
Monday		
Tuesday		
Wednesday		
Thursday		
Friday		
Saturday		

4. (A) For what period of time may an open shelf book be charged out?
   (B) A reserve book?
5. (A) What is the *daily* fine for an overdue book?
   (B) What is the *hourly* fine for an overdue book?
6. Does the library have closed stacks? If so, how do you get books?

Important Terms in Chapter 1

circulation
"closed catalog"
reserve
reference

periodicals
public services
technical services
stacks

2. The Card Catalog and Cataloging Systems

Objectives

After studying this chapter the student shall be able to
- distinguish among microfiche, card and computer catalogs
- distinguish among the three types of catalog units (cards): subject, author, and title
- interpret all the information on the catalog unit for the three types of cards
- use call numbers to locate materials anywhere in the library
- use either Dewey Decimal system or the Library of Congress system to locate materials
- use alphabetical filing rules to locate catalog units

The Catalog

Catalogs contain all the books owned by a particular library. Trying to use the library without referring to the catalog is like looking for the proverbial needle in a haystack. Besides showing what a library owns, the catalog supplies information about each holding. Most libraries catalog their pamphlets, records, tapes, microforms and other resources as well as books. A card catalog is a series of cabinets filled with 3 × 5 cards in drawers.

Some libraries are no longer using a card catalog, but have the same information on microfiche, magnetic tape or CDs. Microfiche catalogs are frequently called COM (computer output microfiche) and are computer-produced. They are updated frequently. Colleges and universities that use COM will probably have COM readers available in many places on the campus outside the library, such as classrooms, dorms, and faculty offices. Other libraries have their catalog on magnetic tape or CD, which require the use of a computer terminal. Libraries locate terminals throughout the library and sometimes in locations outside the library. Libraries that have an on-line catalog (OPAC — On-line Public Access Catalog) may also allow access from remote computers via a modem. Additional information about OPACs will be found in Chapter 3. Libraries with their holdings on computer tapes (database) sometimes print out copies of part of the catalog and have these available for general campus use. These printouts are updated on a regular basis.

The library lists most items in the catalog by subject, by author and by title. Fiction and autobiography, however, usually do not have subject entries. There are two ways to organize the catalog. The "dictionary catalog" organizes all the units (cards) in one alphabetical file. The "divided catalog" is organized in two alphabetical sequences, one for subject units and one for author and title units. These two sequences are clearly labeled, and consultation in both segments may be necessary to determine all listings.

The Catalog Unit

The units in the catalog provide diverse kinds of information. Figure 2.1 illustrates a typical Library of Congress (LC) printed *author card* for a book. The author's name is the top line and is printed in a heavier, blacker type. The date, 1922– , indicates the author's year of birth. In this example the *ed.* after the author's name shows that Harvey Seymour Gross is the editor of this book.

The next line is indented and contains the title of the book, *The Structure of Modern Verse*. The subtitle of the book is *Modern Essays on Prosody*. The next entry indicates that this book was edited by and has both an introduction and a commentary written by Harvey Gross. The following piece of information deals with the edition, in this case a *revised* edition. Next is the information about the publication of the book; first the city of publication, *New York*, second the publishing company, *Ecco Press*, and last the date of publication, 1979.

Figure 2.1

PN
1042   **Gross, Harvey Seymour,** 1922-   ed.
G7   The structure of verse : modern essays on prosody / edited
1979   with an introd. and commentary by Harvey Gross. — Rev. ed.
          — New York : Ecco Press, 1979.
              293 p. ; 24 cm.

              Bibliography: p. 287-290.
              SUMMARY: Essays by Eliot, Pound, Roethke, Graves, Fussell, and others
          on prosody, meter, rhythm—the art of making verses.
              ISBN 0-912946-58-X : $17.50

              1. Versification—Addresses, essays, lectures. [1. Versification.   2. Poetics
          Addresses, essays, lectures]   I. Title.

          PN1042.G7   1979   808.1   78-6781
                                                                              MARC

              Library of Congress   78   AC

All author cards provide information in the following order (* — if applicable):

1. author's name
2. birth and death dates*
3. title
4. subtitle*
5. coauthor's name*
6. notes on editor, compiler, illustrator*
7. edition number*
8. place of publication
9. publishing company
10. date of publication or copyright

A very important item of information on the card is the call number, in the upper left hand corner next to the author's name. This number allows retrieval of the materials.

Unfortunately most students do not pay attention to the rest of the information on the card. Some information can be very useful in selecting books before going to the shelves. The line after the publication data contains the collation, which is information about number of pages in the book (293) and the height of the book (24 centimeters). At first glance the height of a book might seem irrelevant, but this may be a vital clue to locating a book. Some libraries store oversized books on special shelves.

The card in Figure 2.1 also has several notes. This book has a bibliography (on pages 287 to 290), and this card includes a summary of the contents of the book. Information in these notes can be particularly useful if the student needs a book that specifically includes a bibliography, illustrations, maps or other resources. The numbered items near the bottom of the card are often referred to as added entries. They include all the subject headings assigned to this book (those with Arabic numbers) plus other cards in the catalog for the title, coauthor or series (those with Roman numerals). This book by Gross has two subject headings assigned to it and therefore will have two different subject heading cards in the catalog. There will be an additional card for the title.

Card A in Figure 2.2 is an example of a *title card*. Note how the title of the book has been added to the card above the author's name. Subject cards can easily be distinguished from author, title or series cards because the subject will be typed in all capital letters or in red ink.

Cards B and C in Figure 2.2 are examples of *subject cards*. Note how the subject headings have been typed in capital letters above the author's name, one card for each subject heading assigned to this book.

The last line of numbers on the card (see Figure 2.1) includes three sets of numbers; the first is the Library of Congress classification number, the second is the Dewey Decimal classification number, and the third is the Library of Congress card number (used for ordering cards from LC).

In the early 1980s the Library of Congress stopped printing cards. Some book publishers, jobbers and dealers print cards and supply them with the books. Libraries that are members of OCLC (see Chapter 14) have their cards printed by computers at OCLC. The cards supplied by OCLC look as though they have been typed on a typewriter. They will resemble those illustrated in Figure 2.3, which is a complete set of cards, including the main entry (A), subject card (B), title card (C) and a series card (D). Some libraries may use other computerized systems to produce similar cards.

The Call Number

Libraries use either the Dewey Decimal Classification System or the Library of Congress Classification System. The call number, in the

Figure 2.2

PN
1042
G7
1979

The structure of a verse.

Gross, Harvey Seymour, 1922-   ed.
    The structure of verse : modern essays on prosody / edited
with an introd. and commentary by Harvey Gross. — Rev. ed.
— New York : Ecco Press, 1979.
    293 p. ; 24 cm.

A

PN
1042
G7
1979

POETICS - ADDRESSES, ESSAYS, LECTURES.

Gross, Harvey Seymour, 1922-   ed.
    The structure of verse : modern essays on prosody / edited
with an introd. and commentary by Harvey Gross. — Rev. ed.

B

PN
1042
G7
1979

VERSIFICATION - ADDRESSES, ESSAYS, LECTURES.

Gross, Harvey Seymour, 1922-   ed.
    The structure of verse : modern essays on prosody / edited
with an introd. and commentary by Harvey Gross. — Rev. ed.
— New York : Ecco Press, 1979.
    293 p. ; 24 cm.
    Bibliography: p. 287-290.
    SUMMARY: Essays by Eliot, Pound, Roethke, Graves, Fussell, and others
on prosody, meter, rhythm   the art of making verses.
    ISBN 0-912946-58-X : $17.50

    1. Versification—Addresses, essays, lectures. [1. Versification. 2. Poetics
Addresses, essays, lectures]   I. Title.

C

upper left hand corner of the card, shows which system is being used.
A Library of Congress call number begins with one, two or three *letters*
whereas the call number in the Dewey Decimal system starts with a
number. Melvil Dewey devised the decimal system in the 19th century
while a student at Amherst College. The Amherst Library was in disorder (as were most large libraries of the time) and it was impossible to
find specific books. Dewey used a numerical system to arrange the
books and submitted it to the Amherst Library Committee for con-
sideration. Many libraries throughout the world still use his system.

Understanding of the Dewey system helps to find books by browsing and is also helpful in selecting books using the catalog. Dewey divided
all knowledge into nine categories, numbering them 100 through 900,
and put all the general reference works (dictionaries, encyclopedias,
newspapers, etc.) into the category 000. Figure 2.4 shows Dewey's
general system headings.

Each of these general categories is broken down into nine specific
categories and each of these into nine more specific categories. Then,
by adding a decimal point, the system can be expanded continuously.
Figure 2.5 contains an example of the 500 category broken down into
subcategories. For instance, 540 contains Chemistry and Allied
Sciences; 590 contains Zoological Sciences. Subcategory 590 can be

Figure 2.3

BX
4827
S3
G47
1984

Gerrish, B. A. (Brian Albert), 1931-
    A prince of the church : Schleiermacher and
the beginnings of modern theology / B.A.
Gerrish. -- Philadelphia : Fortress Press, c1984.
    79 p. ; 22 cm. -- (The Rockwell lectures ;
1981)
        Bibliography: p. 71-75.
        Includes index.

A

    1. Schleiermacher, Friedrich, 1768-1834--
Addresses, essays, lectures. I. Title.

    II. Series.

                A prince of the church : Schleiermacher and
                    the beginnings of modern theology.
BX
4827
S3
G47
1984

Gerrish, B. A. (Brian Albert), 1931-
    A prince of the church : Schleiermacher and
the beginnings of modern theology / B.A.
Gerrish. -- Philadelphia : Fortress Press, c1984.
    79 p. ; 22 cm. -- (The Rockwell lectures ;
1981)
        Bibliography: p. 71-75.
        Includes index.

B

    1. Schleiermacher, Friedrich, 1768-1834--
Addresses, essays, lectures. I. Title.
II. Series.

                SCHLEIERMACHER, FRIEDRICH, 1768-1834--
                    ADDRESSES, ESSAYS, LECTURES.
BX
4827
S3
G47
1984

Gerrish, B. A. (Brian Albert), 1931-
    A prince of the church : Schleiermacher and
the beginnings of modern theology / B.A.
Gerrish. -- Philadelphia : Fortress Press, c1984.
    79 p. ; 22 cm. -- (The Rockwell lectures ;
1981)

C

        Bibliography: p. 71-75.
        Includes index.

    1. Schleiermacher, Friedrich, 1768-1834--
Addresses, essays, lectures. I. Title.
II. Series.

BX
4827
S3
G47
1984

                The Rockwell lectures ; 1981.

Gerrish, B. A. (Brian Albert), 1931-
    A prince of the church : Schleiermacher and
the beginnings of modern theology / B.A.
Gerrish. -- Philadelphia : Fortress Press, c1984.
    79 p. ; 22 cm. -- (The Rockwell lectures ;
1981)

D

        Bibliography: p. 71075.
        Includes index.

    1. Schleiermacher, Friedrich, 1768-1834--
Addresses, essays, lectures. I. Title.
II. Series.

Figure 2.4

000 General Works
100 Philosophy and Psychology
200 Religion
300 Social Science
400 Language
500 Pure Science
600 Technology (Applied Science)
700 The Arts
800 Literature
900 History

broken down into the types of Zoological Sciences, such as 591 for (general) Zoology and 599 for Mammals. Likewise 599 can be broken down by using decimals, 599.1 *Monotremata* and 599.9 *Hominidae*. Similarly the .9 categories could be broken down into .91, .92 and so on depending on the specificity needed. A manual is available that contains all the categories in the Dewey system.

As useful as the Dewey system is, it is inefficient for large libraries. Around the turn of the century the Library of Congress, which used no real classification system, was chaotic. Users could not access many materials. Many other materials were hopelessly lost. In 1899 Herbert Putnam was appointed librarian of Congress and began an effort to get the library's materials in order. A study showed that the Dewey system was ineffectual in dealing with such a large library. The staff and other librarians continued devising a classification system that would be usable with the library's unorganized and rapidly growing collection.

Besides devising the classification system for the Library of Congress, Putnam felt that it was not really necessary for every library to read and catalog the same books. He thought it would be preferable for the Library of Congress do that work and then share its work with other libraries. He also offered to sell copies of the cards printed by the Library of Congress for its own collection. Librarians eagerly received his ideas since cataloging and card production are time-consuming tasks. Libraries worldwide use the cataloging and card copy produced by the Library of Congress.

The Library of Congress system uses one of 21 letters of the alphabet as the first letter of the classification number. A second or third letter may be added to make up the first part of the classification or call number. Using letters provides more categories than the Dewey

Figure 2.5

500 Pure Science
510 Mathematics
520 Astronomy and Allied Science
530 Physics
540 Chemistry and Allied Science
550 Science of the Earth and the other worlds
560 Paleontology—Paleozoology
570 Life Sciences
580 Botanical Sciences
590 Zoological Sciences
    591 Zoology
    592 Invertebrates (animal plankton and neuston)
    593 Protozoa and other simple animals
    594 Mollusca and molluscoidea
    595 Other invertebrates
    596 Chordata Vertebrata (Craniata, vertebrates)
    597 Cold Blooded vertebrates—Pisces (fish)
    598 Aves (birds)
    599 Mammalia (Mammals)
        599.1 Momotremata
        599.2 Marsupialia
        599.3 Unguiculata
        599.4 Chiroptera (bats)
        599.5 Cetacea and Sirenia
        599.6 Paenungulata
        599.7 Fernungulata and Tubulidentata
        599.8 Primates
        599.9 Hominidae (humankind and forebears)

system. The system leaves some letters unassigned to provide for un-discovered knowledge. Other letters like O are not used because they may be easily confused with the number 0 (zero). The second line of the LC call number is a number from 1 to 9999. Often these two lines make up the subject part of the call number.

    Figure 2.6 contains the general categories in the LC system. For example, B contains Philosophy, Psychology and Religion and N contains Fine Arts. Fine Arts, N, can be further subdivided by adding a second letter. For example, in Figure 2.7 NA is Architecture and NE is

Figure 2.6

A General Works

B Philosophy, Psychology, Religion

C History—Auxiliary Sciences

D History—Except America

E-F America

G Geography, Anthropology, Sports

H Social Sciences

J Political Science

K Law

L Education

M Music

N Fine Arts

P Language

Q Science

R Medicine

S Agriculture, Plant and Animal Industry

T Technology

U Military Sciences

V Naval Sciences

Z Bibliography, Libraries, Library Science

Figure 2.7

N   Fine Arts

NA Architecture

NB Sculpture

NC Graphic Arts, Drawing and Design

ND Painting

NE Engraving

NK Art applied to Industry, Decoration and Ornament

Engraving. Also further categories can be devised by adding numbers on the next line, as illustrated in Figure 2.8 (this figure shows just the beginning of the NE tables). As is the case in the Dewey system, the LC system has manuals describing all the various categories.

To review, the first line of the Dewey number and (generally) the first two lines of the LC number refer to the topic of the book. These call numbers then provide a means of keeping all the books on the same topic in the same section of the library. Both systems also include another line of the call number for the particular author found under the subject indicated. The author line starts with the first letter of the author's last name (see Figure 2.1 again: G for Gross). This letter then may be followed by a number of additional letters. These numbers provide finer discriminations, that may be necessary in extremely large libraries but will not be further discussed here. Thus the first line of the

Figure 2.8

NE ENGRAVING
  1 Periodicals
    10 Yearbooks
    20 Encyclopedias
    25 Dictionaries
    30 Directories
       Exhibitions (by Place)
    40 International
    45 Others
       Museums. Collections
       Public (Art Galleries, Print Departments, etc.)
    53   American
    55   European
       Private
    57   United States
    59
       Sales Catalogs
    63   Before 1801
    65   Auction catalogs 1801–
    70   Dealers' catalogs 1801–
    75   Publishers' catalogs 1801–

call number in Dewey and usually the first two lines in LC denote the subject of the book. The next line (often the last line) is the alphabetic listing of authors within that subject. This system makes it convenient to "browse" through the stacks and to find information without using the catalog. The call numbers also can be thought of as the "address" of the book: it tells the user exactly where that specific book can be found in the library.

To locate materials, the call number in the catalog must be matched with the shelf area location. The book's call number must be copied exactly as it appears in the catalog since each item has a unique number. Once the individual becomes familiar with the location of the shelves, a piece of material can be located quickly, since librarians mark the shelves with a label at one or both ends of the stack.

It should be noted that some libraries have an "oversized" book section. Books that are too large for the regular shelves are put in special sections. For example, many art books are oversized and may be found in this section. If the student is unable to locate materials on the shelves, he or she should **ask the librarian.** The librarian will be able to tell the student if a particular book is on reserve, out in circulation or in some special section. Many libraries will recall books in circulation or put a "hold" (held/reserves upon return for the person requesting) on the book; when the book is returned the requesting individual is notified.

Filing Rules — Alphabetizing

An understanding of some of the rules for filing cards in the catalog may facilitate the use of the catalog. Catalogers file cards word by word rather than letter by letter. Thus **New York** comes before **news.** Personal names beginning with **Mac** and **Mc** are interfiled (filed together) as if they were all spelled **Mac.** Words which begin with **mac** (e.g., machete) will be interfiled with the personal names — see Figure 2.9.

If "A," "An" or "The" is the first word of the title, the filer ignores it. If it appears any place in the title other than the first word, it is considered when filing. If the title is in a foreign language and the title begins with the equivalent of "a," "an" or "the" (for example, Der, Das, La, Le), the word is ignored when filing. Cards are filed by the first (top-most) line on the card. It may be the author's name, the title, the subject or the name of the series.

Figure 2.9

MacArthur	McGregor
McClusky	machete
MacDonald	machine
mace	MacIntosh

Words that are commonly abbreviated are filed as if then were spelled out. For example, **St.** is filed as **Street** or **Saint** (as the case may be), **Dr.** as if written **Doctor,** and **U.S.** as if written **United States.** However, since **Mrs.** is not everywhere equated with "mistress," it is filed as **M-R-S,** whereas **Mr.** is filed as if it were **Mister.**

Words which may be written as one word, two words or hyphenated are interfiled. For example, folksong, folk-song or folk song would all be interfiled, as would text book and text-book. Hyphenated words or names are filed as separate words except when the first word is a prefix: **bull-dog** is filed as two words, **anti-semitism** or **pre-raphaelite** are filed as one.

Numerals and numbers are filed as spoken; thus **1910** is nineteen ten and **VII** is seven.

Initials and acronyms are filed before words beginning with the same letter, and each letter is filed as if it were a word. Thus **FORTRAN** (think of it as F.O.R.T.R.A.N.) comes before **Fables**.

A personal name comes before a subject, e.g., **Wood, Joseph** comes before **WOOD**.

Exercises for Chapter 2

1. Look up the subject headings SNOW and SUMMER in LCSH. Record all headings, subheadings, notes, etc. that are listed. Record, if any, the BT, RT, NT, etc. headings.
2. Using the card catalog find the call numbers of the following books. Record the call numbers and then locate the books on the shelves.
   (A) *McGraw-Hill Encyclopedia of Science and Technology*
   (B) *Oxford English Dictionary*
   (C) *World Almanac and Book of Facts*
   (D) *Guide to the Presidency*
   (E) *Famous First Facts*
3. Match the following lines of a catalog card with the type of card it is. Place the letter preceding the type of card in the space provided to the left of the line of the catalog card.

Line of Catalog Card	*Type of Card*
_____ Thomas Jefferson	a. author unit
_____ Jefferson, Thomas	b. title unit
_____ JEFFERSON, THOMAS	c. subject unit

4. Using figures 2.4 and 2.5, give the most specific call number you can for the following books:
   (A) *Basic Astronomy*
   (B) *Introduction to Human Anatomy*
   (C) *The Great Apes of Africa*
   (D) *Encyclopedia Americana*
5. Using figures 2.6, 2.7 and 2.8, give the most specific category you can find for the following books:
   (A) *Custer's Last Stand*

Figure 2.10

Weiss, Peg.
    Kandinsky in Munich : the formative Jugendstil years / by Peg
Weiss. — Princeton, N.J. : Princeton University Press, c1979.

    xxi, 268 p., ₁48₁ leaves of plates : ill. (some col.) ; 23 cm.

    Bibliography: p. ₁217₁-244.
    Includes index.
    ISBN 0-691-03934-8 : $30.00

    1. Kandinsky, Wassily, 1866-1944.   2. Art nouveau—Germany, West—Munich.   I. Title.

ND699.K3W43   759.7   78-51203
                                                        MARC

    Library of Congress   78

(B) *A History of American Education*
(C) *Paintings of Pablo Picasso*
(D) *Early Copper Engravings*
(E) *Pediatric Surgery*
(F) *New York Times Encyclopedia of Sports*
6. The following questions should be answered by consulting the catalog unit reproduced in Figure 2.10.
  (A) What is the publication date?
  (B) In what city was this book published?
  (C) What is the LC call number?
  (D) What is the author's name?
  (E) What is the price of this book?
  (F) How many subject headings have been assigned to this book?
  (G) What is the title of this book?
  (H) Does this book have illustrations?
  (I) What is the Dewey subject assigned to this book?
  (J) Who published this book?

Important Terms in Chapter 2

microfiche	*"see" references*
COM	*subject heading*
cross-reference	*"see also" reference*
LC subject headings	*Dewey system*
catalog	*OPAC*

Important Books for Chapter 2

American Library Association. ALA *Filing Rules.* Chicago: American Library Association, 1980.

_____. *ALA Rules for Filing Catalog Cards,* 2nd ed. Prep. by ALA Editorial committee. Subcommittee on the ALA Rules for Filing Catalog Cards. Pauline A. Seely, chairman and editor. Chicago: American Library Association, 1968.

Comaromi, John P., ed., and Margaret J. Warren, asst. ed. *Manual on the Use of the Dewey Decimal Classification,* 19th ed. Albany, N.Y.: Forest Press/Lake Placid Education Foundation, 1980. The 20th edition, 1993, is also available on CD-ROM from OCLC (the 120th year celebration).

Dewey, Melvil. *A Classification and Subject Index, for Cataloging and Arranging the Books and Pamphlets of a Library.* New York: Gordon Press, 1979. (Reprint of the 1876 ed. published in Amherst, MA.)

Jefferson, Thomas. *Thomas Jefferson's Library: A Catalog with the Entries in His Own Hand.* Edited by James Gilreath and Douglas L. Wilson. Washington, Library of Congress: GPO, 1989.

United States. Library of Congress. Subject Cataloging Division. *Classification; Classes A–Z.* Washington, DC: GPO, 1971– .

3. On-Line Public Access Catalogs

Objectives

After studying this chapter the student shall be able to
- recognize and use Boolean operators
- identify different search procedures for OPACs and card catalogs

Definitions

On-Line—A computer user's ability to interact with the databases.

OPAC—(On-Line Public Access Catalog) The library's computerized catalog that replaces the card catalog and is available to anyone using the library.

CD-ROM—(Compact Disk—Read Only Memory) An optical disk, single sided, with read only memory. Many contain audio or data impressed at time of manufacture. May contain commercial databases.

Remote Access—Communicating with a database via a communication link (phone line).

Dial-Up—Using a telephone line to "dial" or call another computer.

Keyword—A significant word in a title, subject or author's name.

KWIC—(Keyword in Context) A type of indexing that allows searching by any term in any part of the record.

Boolean Operators—(and, or, not, near, with, except, in) Terms used to narrow or broaden searches.

MaRC— (Machine Readable Cataloging) The cataloging of library resources using standardized rules and symbols which various computer programs can read, then print and reorganize the data as desired.

Bar Code— A series of lines varying in thickness, making up a code that is read by an optical scanner.

Gateway— Means of connecting one computer terminal of a network with another terminal or computer of a different network.

Protocol— A set of formats or conventions that allow computers to communicate over data transmission (phone) lines.

Network— An interconnection of computers or nodes by communication facilities (phone lines).

LAN—(Local Area Network) A means of connecting computers that share programs, data, databases, often used in offices, schools, etc.

General Information

Recently libraries have been "closing" their card catalogs and are no longer adding cards. These libraries have a COM catalog (see Chapter 2) or an on-line catalog, usually called an OPAC (On-Line Public Access Catalog). The libraries that have public access catalogs also will have open computer terminals and some form of instruction on how to search the on-line catalog. On-line catalogs can now be found in public libraries, public school libraries (elementary through high school), college and university libraries and special libraries. Many of these on-line catalogs provide more access points in searching than the old card catalog. Libraries that have officially "closed" their card catalog often do not physically remove the cards. This permits a transition period for those people who are learning to use computers. Some libraries *must* keep their old card catalogs, since the old cards are not yet stored in the computer database. Both card catalog and database must be consulted. If there is a power failure or a computer malfunction occurs, the card catalog serves as a backup.

Libraries which have an OPAC have generally automated (computerized) all the library's operations: circulation, cataloging, periodical check-in and binding, reserves and other daily library procedures. All the daily operations then appear in the public catalog. Thus, when searching the catalog the student is informed of the status of the item, such as "on the shelf," "out in circulation," "on reserve," "on order," or

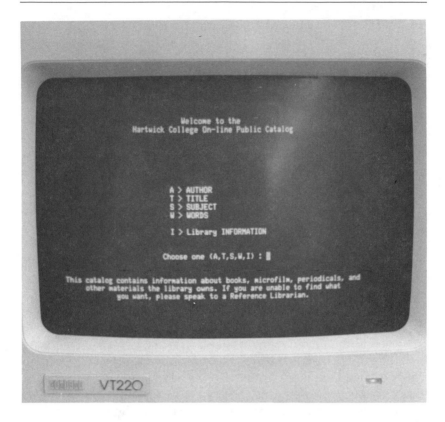

A main menu for starting a search on an OPAC.

"at the bindery." The catalog also shows the latest issue of a periodical that the library has received and on some systems what date the next issue is expected to arrive. Some circulation systems will generate overdue notices to remind patrons that books should be returned.

Some OPACs allow remote access, that is, if you know the protocol it is possible dial-up the library computer from a computer outside the library. Then one searches the library's catalog as if you were in the library. Some OPACs have a "gateway" or system allowing the user to access other computers or remote periodical indexes. There is sometimes a charge for using this type of "gateway." Some libraries have bulletin boards or newsletters with information about the school or community that can be accessed from the OPAC "gateway."

Libraries using OPACs generally have printed instructions at the terminal and provide on-line help. If the student has difficulty while searching, a help command gives additional onscreen instructions. Some terminals attached to the OPAC will have printers. The individuals borrowing from libraries using OPACs will need a special card that will have a bar code.

Searching the OPAC

OPACs allow searching by author, title, and subject just as with the card catalog, CD-ROM or COM catalog. In each case it is necessary to following the directions for that particular system. Some systems use a series of menus from which the user selects the desired type of search. Other systems require the user to type in a command to select the type of desired search. Often a mnemonic system is employed. Because the computer can read all the words in each entry it is possible to provide additional points of access. It is possible to do a keyword search, one in which the computer looks for a word anyplace it appears in the author index, title index or subject index. Some systems allow free text keyword searching, that is the systems searches for that word anyplace in the record. Some systems also allow the use of Boolean searching in the keyword search and may provide searching by ISBN, ISSN or OCLC number. Some systems allow searching by call number, a means of browsing the shelves without going to the shelf. This is particularly useful if the library has closed stacks. Some systems allow searches to be revised without starting over, a blessing for those who can't type. Some systems allow the limiting of a search by date, a range of dates, or by language.

When doing an author search, the author's name should be searched last name first, just as in the card catalog. It is generally not necessary to put commas between names. One may enter just the last name or as many letters of the last name as are known (a truncated or shortened term). Some systems require the entry of a special symbol to show a truncated entry, e.g., "?," "*" or "#." For example it is possible to enter **Green?** The system will then display *all* the authors whose last name begins with those letters and the student can then choose the desired entry. For example—Green, Greenblat, Greene, Greenstone, Greentree, etc. When searching by author, it is sometimes possible to enter alternative spellings using Boolean operators and doing just one search, e.g., Green or Greene. This is preferable to using the truncated search as it eliminates all except the two possible spellings of the name.

Title searches also allow the student to enter as many words as are known and the OPAC will display on the screen *all* the books that start with those words (see Figure 3.1 titles beginning with the word "**beach**" and with the words "**little house**"). The desired title can then be selected from the list. It is sometimes permissible to use truncated words in title searches.

Figure 3.1

Search: T = BEACH

LINE #   -TITLE- -

1	Beach and Sea Animals
2	Beach at St. Addressee
3	Beach Ball
4	The Beach Before Breakfast
5	Beach Bird
6	Beach Birds
7	The Beach Book and the Beach Bucket
8	The Beach Boys

(MORE)

Search: T = LITTLE HOUSE

LINE #   -TITLE- -

1	The Little House
2	The Little House; a new math story game
3	The Little House Books
4	The Little House Cookbook: frontier foods from Laura
5	Little House in the Big Woods
6	Little House in the Ozarks
7	A Little House of Your Own
8	Little House on the Prairie

(MORE)

Subject searches may present the most difficulty as some systems require that the subject entered match *exactly* with Library of Congress subject headings. Incorrect subject headings may lead to no matches. Also, if the student has not consulted LCSH (Library of Congress Subject Headings, see Chapter 4) guessing correct headings is even more difficult. Some systems are "kinder" ("user friendly") than others and instead of saying "no match," provide an alphabetical list of terms that surround the heading entered. Some systems also provide cross references and show the number of entries for each cross reference. This feature allows the student to choose other subjects without rekeying the search.

Some systems allow the student to combine the author's name and the book title in one search. If the author's name is common or the author has published many books (e.g. Shakespeare) this option provides fewer "hits" and is more likely to display the desired title with fewer steps.

Keyword searches often produce the most number of entries and so it is necessary to devise a good search strategy. See the following section on Boolean searching.

In many ways OPACs are just elaborate card catalogs and we should not expect more than they can provide. Some systems display a message "no match" on your search term; the same result is sometimes obtained when searching a card catalog. Other systems are more helpful, providing cross references and other words that appear before and after the search term entered. Some card catalogs also provide cross references and by flipping through the cards in a card catalog, we, of course, find the words before and after the term searched. Librarians say that many students spend more time using the OPAC than a card catalog. An OPAC is constantly developing and changing.

Boolean Searching

In those OPACs that include Boolean search capabilities the Boolean operators generally include "and," "or," and "not." Boolean searches can be done in other types of databases such as periodical indexes on CD-ROM or via on-line vendors such as DIALOG or BRS. These systems add additional operators such as "with" and "near."

The use of the "and" operator serves to narrow a search by looking for entries that contain **both** terms, e.g., North "and" South. The "or" operator serves to enlarge the search by looking for entries that contain **either** of the terms, North "or" South. The "not" search narrows a search by eliminating from the search all citations with the undesired term, North "not" South. The "not" operator should be used with caution as it might eliminate desired entries (see Figure 3.2).

Figure 3.2

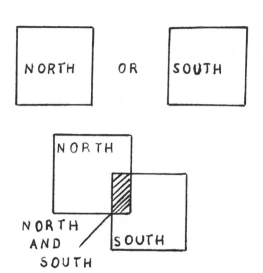

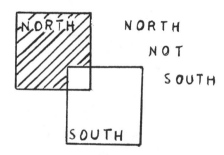

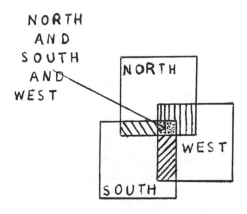

Exercises for Chapter 3

1. Do an author search for Jean M. Auel.
   (A) First try just her last name.
   (B) Record (or print) the results.
   (C) Try her full name.
   (D) Was there a difference in the results?
   (E) Was there a difference in the time it took for the system to search?
2. Do a title search for Jean M. Auel's book *Clan of the Cave Bear.*
   (A) Try the search first using just the first word of the title. Record (or print) your results.
   (B) Try the search again using the first couple of words of the title. How did your results differ from previous title search?
3. Suppose you did not know the exact title of the book in question 2 but did know "Cave Bear" was in the title.
   (A) How would you search for this title? Try your solution.
   (B) Did it work? If not, can you give an explanation?
4. Try a subject search for books on cave dwellers.
   (A) What subject did you enter? Was it successful?
   (B) Record (or print) your results. How would you use information from this search to find additional books?
   (C) Call up a complete record from this search. What is its status?
   (D) Does the library have more than one copy? If you are using a public library system, does the system show locations by branch libraries?
5. If the system you are using allows Boolean searching, search Auel *and* Bear.
   (A) Try various combinations of the books by Auel, using various words in the titles. Record (or print) your results.
   (B) Try other combinations that are of interest to you. What did you discover?

Important Terms for Chapter 3

OPAC	CD-ROM
keyword	*Boolean operators*
bar code	*network*
LAN	*user friendly*
truncated	

Important Books for Chapter 3

Crawford, Walt, et al. *Bibliographic Displays in the On-Line Catalog.* Boston: G.K. Hall, 1986.

Dial-In. An annual guide to library online public access catalogs in North America. Westport, CT: Meckler, 1991– .

Dictionary of Computing. 3rd ed. New York: Oxford University Press, 1990.

Fayen, Emily G. *The On-Line Catalog: Improving Public Access to Library Materials.* Boston: G. K. Hall, 1983.

Glossbrenner, Alfred. *The Complete Handbook of Personal Computer Communications.* 3rd ed. New York: St. Martin's Press, 1989.

Matthews, Joseph R. *Access to On-Line Catalogs.* 2nd ed. New York: Neal Schuman, 1985.

Peters, Thomas. *The Online Catalog: A Critical Examination of Public Use.* Jefferson, NC: McFarland, 1991.

4. Subject Headings

Objectives

After studying this chapter the student shall be able to
- use *Library of Congress Subject Headings*
- find correct subject headings for a particular topic
- use various forms of cross references correctly

General Information

Often, students looking for material in the library do not have specific titles or authors in hand and need to use subject headings instead. This is particularly true during the early stages of a search. Frequently, students guess the appropriate heading to use. A proper and specific subject heading is essential for the efficient use of the card catalog, on-line catalog (OPAC), CD-ROM indexes and catalogs, and periodical indexes. Using a heading that seems logical but is inappropriate wastes effort, especially when using OPACs and CD products. For example, searching for information on the battles of the American Civil War, one might use initially the heading **Civil War**. Titles about the Civil War are found more appropriately under **United States — History — Civil War, 1861–1865**.

The dates of events are also important since citations are arranged chronologically within groups. Thus entries **United States — History — Revolution, 1775–1783** and **United States — History — Colonial Period, ca. 1600–1774** both appear before the Civil War entry because

Figure 4.1.
Library of Congress Subject Headings

Here are entered works on the methods and techniques employed in conducting soil surveys, and reports of individual surveys. For the latter the heading may be subdivided by place; in such cases an additional subject entry is made under the heading Soils—{local subdivision}. e.g. 1. Soils—Hawaii. 2. Soil surveys—Hawaii. For soil surveys on a special topic, the additional subject entry is made under the special topic, e.g. 1. Acid soils—Hawaii. 2. Soil surveys—Hawaii.
    BT Surveys
Soil-surveys
    NT Aerial photography in soil surveys
Soil surveys
  — Geophysical methods
    UF Geophysical methods in soil surveys
    BT Geophysics
Soil-surveys
  — Geophysical methods
    NT Seismic refraction method
Soil temperature *(May Subd Geog)*
    {S594.5}
    BT Heat budget (Geophysics)
       Soil physics
       Temperature
Soil testing
    USE Soils—Testing
Soil texture *(May Subd Geog)*
    {S592.35}
Soil trafficability
    USE Trafficability
Soil treatment of wastewater
    USE Land treatment of wastewater
Soil types
    USE Soils—Classification
Soil ventilation
    USE Soil aeration
Soil warming
    USE Soil heating
Soilborne infection *(May Subd Geog)*
    {RA642.S6}
    UF Infection, Soil-borne
       Soil-borne infection
    BT Communicable diseases
       Diseases—Transmission
       Infection
       Soil microbiology
Soilborne plant diseases *(May Subd Geog)*
    {SB732.87}
    UF Soil-borne plant diseases
    BT Plant diseases
    RT Soil microbiology
Soilless agriculture
    USE Hydroponics
Soilless culture
    USE Hydroponics
Soils *(May Subd Geog)*
    {S590-599}
Here are entered works on natural soils. Works on plant growing media which include both natural soils and artificial media are entered under Plant growing media. Works on growing media which do not contain natural soils are entered under Plant growing media, Artificial. Works on growing media for potted plants are entered under Potting soils.
    UF Field crops—Soils
       Mold, Vegetable
       Mould, Vegetable
       Vegetable mold
    BT Agriculture
       Geology, Economic
       Plant growing media
    RT Agricultural chemistry
       Land capability for agriculture
    SA headings beginning with the word Soil and subdivision Soils *under specific plants*, e.g. Fruit—Soils; Rice—Soils
    NT Acid soils
       Alfisols
       Alkali lands
       Black cotton soil
       Burning of land

Calcareous soils
Chernozem soils
Clay
Clay soils
Claypan soils
Corn—Soils
Crops and soils
Desert soils
Duricrusts
Ferralsols
Fluvisols
Forage plants—Soils
Forest soils
Frozen ground
Histosols
Humus
Hydromorphic soils
Irrigation
Leaf-mold
Loam soils
Mine soils
Mountain soils
Mulching
Particles
Peat soils
Podzol
Potting soils
Problem soils
Red soils
Rhizosphere
Sandy loam soils
Sierozem
Smonitza
Soil amendments
Soil profiles
Solonetz soils
Tillage
Tundra soils
Variable charge soils
Vertisols
Volcanic soils
Volusia soils
— Abstracts
    USE Soil science—Abstracts
— Aeration
    USE Soil aeration
— Age
    {S592.185 (General)}
    {S599-S599.9 (Local)}
    UF Age of soils
       Soil age
— Agricultural chemical content
    {QH541.5.S6 (Soil ecology)}
    {S592.6.A34 (Agriculture)}
    {TD879.A35 (Soil pollution)}
    BT Agricultural chemicals
— Air content
    USE Soil air
— Aluminum content
    UF Aluminum in soils
    BT Aluminum
— Ammonium content
    BT Ammonium
— Analysis
    {S593}
    UF Analysis of soils
    NT Bacteriology, Agricultural
       Soil micromorphology
       Soils—Composition
— Arsenic content
    UF Arsenic in soils
    BT Arsenic
— Bacteriology
    USE Soil microbiology
— Barium content
    UF Barium in soils
    BT Barium
— Bibliography
    USE Soil science—Bibliography
— Boron content
    UF Boron in soils

    BT Boron
— Cadmium content
    BT Cadmium
— Calcium content
    UF Calcium in soils
    BT Calcium
    NT Soils—Gypsum content
— Capillarity
    USE Soil capillarity
— Carbohydrate content
    {S592.6.C34}
    BT Carbohydrates
       Humus
— Carbon content
    UF Carbon in soils
    BT Carbon
— Carbonate content
    UF Carbonates in soils
    BT Carbonates
— Chlorine content
    UF Chlorine in soils
    BT Chlorine
— Classification
    {S592.16 (General)}
    {S599-S599.9 (Local)}
    UF Soil classification
       Soil types
— Cobalt content
    UF Cobalt in soils
    BT Cobalt
— Collected works
    USE Soil science—Collected works
— Color
    {S592.4}
    UF Color of soils
— Composition
    UF Soil composition
    BT Agricultural chemistry
       Soils—Analysis
    RT Soil mineralogy
    SA Soils—Magnesium content; Soils—Potassium content; *and similar headings*
    NT Humus
       Soil science in archaeology
       Soils—Magnesium content
       Soils—Nickel content
       Soils—Potassium content
       Soils, Salts in
— Consolidation
    USE Soil consolidation
— Copper content
    UF Copper in soils
    BT Copper
— Creep
    UF Slow flowage
    BT Mass-wasting
       Materials—Creep
       Soil mechanics
    RT Solifluction
    NT Soil consolidation
— Density
    UF Soil density
    BT Soil physics
       Specific gravity
    NT Plants, Effect of soil compaction on
       Swelling soils
— Disinfection
    USE Soil disinfection
— Effect of radiation on
    UF Soils, Effect of radiation on
    BT Radiation
— Electric properties
— Fertilization
    USE Fertilizers
       Soil fertility
— Fertilizer movement
    UF Movement of fertilizers in soils
    BT Fertilizers
       Soil physics

they precede it in time. Some catalogs contain cross-references to help minimize this problem. These are of two types: the *see* and the *see also* reference, which lists other closely related subjects.

To help find the correct subject heading when cross-references are not available, searchers need to find additional headings. Users should consult one or more special books that help to discover appropriate subject headings. The most comprehensive of these is *Library of Congress Subject Headings* (LCSH), a four-volume work conspicuous by its bright red cover. Well-equipped libraries use this four-volume work as the "bible" of subject headings and often place this work at the card catalog or near the OPAC terminals. Other books of subject headings that are not as comprehensive are the: *Sears List of Subject Headings*; *Subject Cross Reference Guide*; and *Cross Reference Index*.

Libraries also may have books of subject headings for *specific indexes or subjects*. For example: *Thesaurus of Sociological Indexing Terms* and *A to Zoo: Subject Access to Children's Picture Books*.

Consulting such works before using the catalog will save time and frustration and may provide additional headings, more specific or descriptive than the headings originally checked. Some headings, particularly in the *Library of Congress* work, may contain voluminous entries, filling an entire column or more. See Figure 4.1 for the subject **Soils** that continues on to a second full page in LCSH. This means the subject is very broad and the user might consider specifying a narrower topic. This is particularly important in writing term papers. Problems in writing term papers often begin by selecting topics that are too comprehensive.

Using Library of Congress Subject Headings *(LCSH)*

The LCSH is the list of subject headings assigned by the Library of Congress to books in its collection. It reflects the changes and growth in the collection since the development of the LC Classification system in 1898. The 14th edition was published in 1991 and is the first edition to use abbreviations introduced with computer thesaurus in the mid–1980s. The introductory material in the front of volume 1 contains explanations and instruction on how headings are arranged and assigned.

Subject headings may be one word or several words. A one word subject heading is usually a noun, with concepts using the singular form and objects using plural forms:

authorship (concept – singular)
soils (object – plural) (see Figure 4.1)

Two word headings are generally an adjective and a noun and may be inverted, especially if the adjective describes a language or a nationality. In recent years the natural word order is the preferred form except for language, national or ethnic adjectives. Older headings are more likely to be in inverted word order. Examples are:

authorship, disputed
coach horses
churches, Anglican
Camsa language
dramatists, Italian
soilborne infection (see Figure 4.1)

Names of geographic places are usually inverted to put the significant word first, e.g., Michigan, Lake. Headings with more than two words may include conjunctions and prepositional phrases. Headings with reciprocal relations or generally used associated ideas may be combined. Those headings with prepositional phrases may be in the *inverted format*. Examples are:

charity laws and legislation
bites and stings
Antietam, Battle of, 1862
bachelor of arts degree
technology and civilization

Place names may also be used as subject headings and subheadings. Over the years the format for place names has changed as have the rules used to assign subject headings for place names. In addition, many places have changed their names. Thus place names in card catalogs and even in OPACs are inconsistent and diligent searching is necessary to locate all desired information. An example of a geographic heading that is confusing for users of any type of the catalog is **George, Lake** (not **Lake George**) but **Lake George Region.** Examples of place name changes include colonies that have become independent nations and changed their name, territory conquered in war resulting in city or country name changes, name changes in cities when governments change such as St. Petersburg–Petrograd–Leningrad, a city known by three different names this century. In 1991, the citizens voted to change the name back to St. Petersburg.

Cross references are always helpful in directing students from incorrect headings to correct headings. Also helpful are cross references between similar headings or between broad and narrow headings. Many libraries, catalogs, and indexes use *see* and *see also* headings. The *see* reference directs the student from an incorrect heading to a correct heading. The 11th edition of LCSH and many computer thesauri have substituted the term *use* for *see.* The function remains the same, directing the user to the correct heading.

The *see also* (or SA) reference directs the student to other headings that are related. Recent computer thesauri and LCSH are supplementing the *see also* reference with additional breakdowns as follows:

RT = related term
BT = broader term
NT = narrower term
UF = use from, a cross reference from the *use* reference

The inclusion of the UF in a list means that terms designated with UF are *not* good subject headings and should not be used when searching.

In Figure 4.1 for the subject heading **soils,** note that UF references include *Field crops — Soils; Mold, Vegetable; Mould, Vegetable;* and *Vegetable mold.* These headings are not to be used and if the user looked, for example, under *Field crops — Soil,* LCSH says *use — soils.* The BT or broader terms include *Agriculture; Geology, Economic;* and *Plant growing media.* The RT or related term are *Agricultural chemistry* and *Land capability for agriculture.* The note for SA (see also) says "headings beginning with the word *Soil* and subdivision *Soils* under specific plants, e.g., *Fruit — Soils; Rice — Soils.*" The list for NT or narrower term is long with nearly 50 entries, ranging from *Acid soils* to *Volusia soils.* For examples of a *use* reference see Figure 4.1 **Soils** — *Aeration* USE *Soil aeration* and **Soils** — *Abstracts* USE *Soil science — Abstracts.*

LCSH also includes a variety of notes with the subject headings and their subdivisions. Often the beginning or subject class number (see Chapter 2) of the call number is included. See Figure 4.1 **Soils** and note the call number of S590-599. Also note that there are call numbers included with some of the subdivisions, (see Figure 4.1, middle column) e.g. **Soils** — Age is S592.5S6 (Soil ecology). With this information the student can go to the shelves and browse to see which books the library has on the subject. Having part of the call number is also useful with those OPACs that have a call number browse search option. Another type of note that may be included is a scope note — one that explains what is included or excluded in that particular subject heading. See Figure 4.1 for **Soils,** note that this heading says (*May Subd Geog*) and includes a scope note that begins "Here are entered works on natural soils. Works on plant growing media. . . ."

There are generally four types of subdivisions used by Library of Congress:

1. topical — ones that limit the concept
   semiconductors — failures
2. form — includes the literary form
   addresses, essays, lectures
   periodical
   abstracts
   collected works (Figure 4.1)
3. chronological — shows time period(s)
   Sicily — civilization — 15th century
   Sri Lanka — history — 1505-1948
4. geographical — shows places
   public buildings — Spain

The countries that are exceptions to this rule are the United States, Canada, Russia and Great Britain. These countries have more specific breakdowns, using names of states, provinces, regions, constituent countries and republics instead of just the name of the country, e.g. public buildings — Washington, D.C.

Not all possible subdivisions are listed in LCSH. Subdivisions are marked by a dash that eliminates the need to repeat the main heading. If a subdivision has a subdivision there will be two dashes.

Searching the Catalog

If you are searching the subject heading in the card catalog you can browse easily through the cards and find singular and plural forms of the term and other headings beginning with the same word. Subject cards can be identified from other cards in the catalog because the top-most line on the card is typed in capital letters or in red ink. In most OPACs a user starts a subject search from the menu or with a command s = or su =. If you are subject searching in an OPAC instead of in a card catalog the process may be more difficult, depending on the system used. Some OPACs allow free text searching (see Chapter 3). In others the subject term entered into the computer must be an *exact* match to a Library of Congress subject heading. Problems could be singular vs. plural forms of the word, inverted terms, etc. Searching any catalog by subject is limited by the number of subject terms assigned and by the imprecise use of some headings and the changes in terminology through time.

Exercises for Chapter 4

1. Using *Library of Congress Subject Headings,* look up the subject **Last Supper.** Record call number, any notes, cross references, subheadings or other subjects beginning with the term **Last Supper.**
2. Using *Library of Congress Subject Headings* find the correct subject heading(s) needed to locate information about the conflicts between the Jews and the Palestinians and or other Arab groups.
3. Using *Library of Congress Subject Headings* locate and record one or two examples of subject headings that use or contain the following:
   (A) chronological subdivisions
   (B) geographical subdivisions
   (C) scope note(s)
   (D) class number(s)
   (E) multiple cross references
4. Using your example in question 3E, trace and record all cross references to BT, NT, RT, SA, UF and USE. Is the example in 3E a topic usable for a term paper? Why or why not?

Important Terms in Chapter 4

cross reference   "RT" reference
"see" reference   "USE" reference
"see also" reference   "UF" reference
"BT" reference   OPAC
"NT" reference   LCSH

Important Books for Chapter 4

Atkins, Thomas V. *Cross Reference Index: A Guide to Search Terms.* New York: Bowker, 1984, 1989.

Booth, Barbara, and Michael Blair. *Thesaurus of Sociological Indexing Terms.* 2nd edition. San Diego, CA, 1989.

Lima, Carolyn W., and John A. Lima. *"A to Zoo" Subject Access to Children's Picture Books.* 3rd ed. New York: R. R. Bowker, 1989.

Markey, Karen. *Subject Searching in Library Catalogs Before and After the Introduction of On-Line Catalogs.* Dublin, OH: OCLC On-Line Corp., 1984.

Sears List of Subject Headings. 14th ed. New York: N. W. Wilson, 1991.

Subject Guide to Books in Print. 5 vols. *Thesaurus.* New York: R. R. Bowker, 1992–1993.

Thesaurus of Psychological Index Terms. 6th ed. Alvin Walker, ed. Arlington, VA: American Psychological Association, 1991.

United States. Library of Congress. Subject Cataloging Division. *Library of Congress Subject Headings.* 14th ed. 1991.

5. Bibliography

Objectives

After studying this chapter the student shall be able to
- distinguish between the two types of bibliography, book length and short lists
- figure out where to find lists of available published books and how to use these lists
- use the *National Union Catalog,* the *Cumulative Book Index* and the *Bibliographic Index* to locate materials
- distinguish between annotated bibliographies and the other types and how to find materials in them
- recognize an appropriate format for writing bibliographies
- locate bibliographies on specific topics

General Information

After defining a topic the writer will find a bibliography an essential part of research. *Webster's Third New International Dictionary of the English Language Unabridged* (1971) defines bibliography as follows:

> 1a: the history, identification, or analytical and systematic description or classification of writings or publications considered as material objects b: the investigation or determination of the relationships of varying texts or multiple editions of a single work or a related group of works—called also *analytic bibliography,*

descriptive bibliography. **2** : a list or catalog, often descriptive or critical notes, of writings related to a particular subject, period or author «a *b*— of modern poetry» «a *b*— of the 17th century»; *also* a list of works *b*— of Walt Whitman» «a publisher's *b*—» **3** : the works, or a list of them, mentioned in a text or consulted by an author in a production of that text—usu. included as an appendix to the work «a *b*— of 40 books and articles» **4** : the study of bibliography or bibliographic methods «an intensive course in *b*—»

Most students are familiar with bibliographies that are citations of the works used by an author in writing a book or paper (see definition 3 above). Yet, bibliographies such as those found in definition 2 are extremely useful to the sophisticated searcher. Libraries have many bibliographies of this type that are invaluable when preparing a list of materials on a topic.

Bibliographies may be book length, containing thousands of entries, or may be only several pages in length. For instance, the *Indians of North and South America* by Carolyn Wolf is a comprehensive bibliography containing over 4,200 sources of information on that topic.

On the other hand, some bibliographies are listings of the works *by* a particular author, some *about* a particular author and some are both. For example the bibliography by Joan Crane, *Willa Cather: A Bibliography,* is just a list of works by Willa Cather. Yet the bibliography by John A. Stoler, *Daniel Defoe: An Annotated Bibliography of Modern Criticism, 1900–1980,* contains a list of works by Defoe *and* a list of critical analysis of Defoe's works. To find these bibliographies in the card catalog one looks under the author's name as a subject. The author's name will be typed in red ink or printed in capital letters. When using an OPAC the student must do a subject search.

Other bibliographies are topical. Subjects or authors' names will be arranged alphabetically. Sometimes the student will find bibliographies that contain both subjects and authors in one alphabetical listing. Another category of bibliographies is determined by geographical area. Some of these contain items about or published in a specific country, while others may be regional or international in scope. Further, a distinction may be made on the time period with which the bibliography deals. For instance, a bibliography might contain only works of Russian authors of the 19th century.

Some bibliographies are detailed lists of other bibliographies. A logical starting point for researching a particular topic is to consult one of these comprehensive bibliographies. Then one should see if the library has or can obtain the most useful ones. There is an extensive section in the card catalog under the subject bibliography that lists most of the bibliographies in the library.

Also, bibliographies can be located under a specific subject heading that has the subheading "bibliography"—for example, air pollution–bibliography contains references to lists of information on air pollution.

The following are books that are either bibliographies or contain useful information about bibliographies.

Books in Print

Books in Print (BIP in library lingo) is a current list of books published by *major* American publishers. Students will find a set in all libraries, book stores and other large stores with a book department. BIP is a listing of books *available for purchase*. This listing could include a book written 50 years ago if it is still available for purchase from the publisher. A book published a year ago that is no longer available for purchase will not be listed. BIP is published annually and the new edition generally is available in the fall.

Books in Print includes scholarly, popular, adult, juvenile, reprint editions and all other types of books, provided they are published or exclusively distributed in the United States and are available to the trade or to the public for single or multiple copy purchase according to the preface to BIP.

BIP has author, title, subject and publisher sections arranged alphabetically. The subject section, *Subject Guide to Books in Print*, is useful in preparing a list of books on a specific topic. The author section is a listing of the authors found in the subject section and the title section is a listing of the titles in the subject section. The publisher volume is a directory of included publishers.

The entries in BIP include the author(s) name(s), title, publisher, date of publication, price of the book, and other ordering information for libraries and book stores. The ordering information is primarily useful for library staff but may be used by the student to order books directly from the publisher.

Library of Congress Catalog of Printed Cards *and the* National Union Catalog

The *Library of Congress Catalog of Printed Cards,* commonly called the *LC Cat,* was first published in 1942 and covered the period 1898 (when cards were first printed) to 1942. Supplements in monthly, quarterly, annual and five-year accumulations have appeared since. The *LC Cat* is a reproduction of the author cards printed by Library of Congress. The *LC Cat* is not a complete list of books at the Library of Congress because the library has books for which cards have never been printed.

Many major libraries in the United States and Canada have supplied the Library of Congress with cards of local, unusual or foreign publications that they have added to their collections. The Library of Congress has interfiled these cards with the cards they have printed, and have thus maintained a "National Union [Card] Catalog" in their Washington, D.C. main building. Each library supplying information has a letter code and the code is added to the card supplied to the Library of Congress. When several libraries supply the same information, the code for each library is added.

In 1956 the Library of Congress changed the scope of the *LC Cat* to include all the entries supplied by other libraries. The title was changed to *The National Union Catalog,* NUC for short, to reflect the change in scope. The codes for all the libraries supplying information are printed after the entry. This helps to locate libraries having a copy of a particular book, which may then be borrowed through interlibrary loan (see Chapter 14).

In 1968 a commercial publisher, Mansell, began a major undertaking, the printing of the *National Union Catalog, Pre–1956 Imprints.* This catalog lists in one alphabet, all the cards printed by the Library of Congress from 1898 to 1956 and all the cards supplied by other libraries up to 1965. All three categories, *LC Cat, NUC,* and *NUC Pre–56 Imprints* are primarily author listings.

In 1950 the Library of Congress began printing a subject approach to *LC Cat* called *Library of Congress, Books—Subjects.* It is published quarterly with annual and five-year accumulations and is arranged by the subject headings assigned to each book by the Library of Congress. The last cumulative set is 1970 to 1974. Annual volumes continued until 1982. Beginning in 1983 the microfiche NUC contains both authors and subjects in one alphabet.

Figure 5.1. Cumulative Book Index

Ireland, Kenneth F.
A classical introduction to modern number theory; [by]
Kenneth Ireland, Michael Rosen. 2nd ed (Graduate
texts in mathematics, 84) 389p 1990 Springer-Verlag
(NY)
ISBN 0-387-97329-X   LC 90-9848

Ireland

Antiquities, Celtic
Laing, L. R. Celtic Britain and Ireland, AD200-800.
£32.50 1990 Irish Acad. Press

Civilization
Weisser, H. Hippocrene companion guide to Ireland.
$14.95 1990 Hippocrene Bks.

Description and travel
Clark, W. Sailing round Ireland. 2nd ed pa £7.95 1990
North-West Bks.
O'Farrell, P. By rail through the heart of Ireland. pa
£7.95 1990 Mercier Press
Distr. in USA by Dufour Eds. pa $16.95
Weisser, H. Hippocrene companion guide to Ireland.
$14.95 1990 Hippocrene Bks.

Views
Browne, F. The genius of Father Browne. 1990 Wolfhound
Press
Distr. in USA by Dufour Eds. $40

Emigration and immigration
Migrations. 1990 Wolfhound Press
Distr. in USA by Dufour Eds. $26

Genealogy
Directories
A Guide to Irish churches and graveyards. 1990
Genealogical

History
To 1172
Hall, R. Viking age archaeology in Britain and Ireland.
pa £3.50 1990 Shire Publs.
Laing, L. R. Celtic Britain and Ireland, AD200-800.
£32.50 1990 Irish Acad. Press
20th century
Dunleavy, J. E. Douglas Hyde. 1991 University of Calif.
Press (Berkeley)

Politics and government
1901-1910
Allen, K. The politics of James Connolly. £16.50 1990
Pluto Press
1910-1921
Allen, K. The politics of James Connolly. £16.50 1990
Pluto Press

Social life and customs
20th century
Donleavy, J. P. A singular country. $18.95 1990 Norton

Irigaray, Luce
Marine lover of Friedrich Nietzsche; translated by Gillian
C. Gill. 190p $35 1991 Columbia Univ. Press
ISBN 0-231-07082-9   LC 90-27059

Cumulative Book Index

The *Cumulative Book Index* (CBI) is an author-title-subject world list of books published in English. It also includes some government documents, pamphlets and privately published items. All entries are in a single alphabetical list. The entries include the author(s), title, publisher, date of publication, price and other information for ordering from the publisher. See Figure 5.1 for a sample entry. Note the many subheadings under the subject **Ireland.** Note that author entries and title entries are interfiled with the subject.

Bibliographic Index

The *Bibliographic Index* is a bibliography of bibliographies. It is a list of bibliographies arranged by subject and where they may be found. If, for example the student desires a bibliography on American Indians, it may be found under that subject, **Indians of North America.** See Figure 5.2 for an example of what the reference looks like. The bibliographies included in *Bibliographic Index* may be a complete book length listing or a bibliography after a journal article, book or chapter of a book.

Figure 5.2. Bibliographic Index

Indians of Central America—*cont.*

Ethnology

See Indians of Central America

Implements

Lewenstein, Suzanne M. Stone tool use at Cerros; the ethnoarchaeological and use-wear evidence. University of Tex. Press 1987 p205-20

Industries

Lewenstein, Suzanne M. Stone tool use at Cerros; the ethnoarchaeological and use-wear evidence. University of Tex. Press 1987 p205-20

Belize

Lewenstein, Suzanne M. Stone tool use at Cerros; the ethnoarchaeological and use-wear evidence. University of Tex. Press 1987 p205-20

Indians of Mexico

Las Tesis de la ENAH; ensayo de sistematización; coordinadores, Agustín Avila [et al.]. Instituto Nacional de Antropología & Hist. 1988 179p

Antiquities

Ancient Chalcatzingo; edited by David C. Grove. University of Tex. Press 1987 p550-62

Palenque Round Table (6th: 1986). Sixth Palenque Round Table, 1986; Merle Greene Robertson, general editor; Virginia M. Fields, volume editor. (Palenque Round Table series, v8) University of Okla. Press 1990 p333-55

Art

Indice bibliográfico sobre artesanías. Programa de Artesanías & Culturas Populares (Mex.) 1988 282p

Ethnology

See Indians of Mexico

History

Indice bibliográfico sobre artesanías. Programa de Artesanías & Culturas Populares (Mex.) 1988 282p

Industries

Indice bibliográfico sobre artesanías. Programa de Artesanías & Culturas Populares (Mex.) 1988 282p

Legends

Scheffler, Lilian. Indice bibliográfico sobre tradición oral. Programa de Artesanías & Culturas Populares (Mexico) 1988 139p

Yucatan

Clendinnen, Inga. Ambivalent conquests; Maya and Spaniard in Yucatan, 1517-1570. (Cambridge Latin American studies, 61) Cambridge Univ. Press 1987 p228-37

Indians of North America

Amusements

See Indians of North America—Social life and customs

Antiquities

Boldurian, A. T. Lithic technology at the Mitchell Locality of Blackwater Draw: a stratified Folsom site in eastern New Mexico. *Plains Anthropol* 35:111-15 S '90

Hofman, J. L. and others. Shifting sands: a Folsom-Midland assemblage from a campsite in Western Texas. *Plains Anthropol* 35:250-3 Ag '90

Thurmond, J. P. Late paleoindian utilization of the Dempsey Divide on the Southern Plains. *Plains Anthropol* 35:55-60 O '90

Architecture

Cable, Carole. Hopi and Zuni Indian architecture; a bibliography. (Architecture series, bibliography A-2380) Vance Bibls. 1990 6p

Biography

Schaaf, Gregory. Wampum belts & peace trees; George Morgan, native Americans, and revolutionary diplomacy. Fulcrum 1990 p261-72 annot

Burial

See Indians of North America—Mortuary customs

Culture

See Indians of North America

Customs

See Indians of North America—Social life and customs

Ethnology

See Indians of North America

Food

Theodoratus, R. J. Loss, transfer, and reintroduction in the use of wild plant foods in the Upper Skagit Valley. *Northwest Anthropol Res Notes* 23:50-2 Spr '89

Government relations

Schaaf, Gregory. Wampum belts & peace trees; George Morgan, native Americans, and revolutionary diplomacy. Fulcrum 1990 p261-72 annot

Health and hygiene

Garro, L. C. Continuity and change: the interpretation of illness in an Anishinaabe (Ojibway) community. *Cult Med Psychiatr* 14:450-4 D '90

Juvenile literature

Norton, D. E. Teaching multicultural literature in the reading curriculum. *Read Teach* 44:38-40 S '90

Languages

Zigmond, Maurice L., and others. Kawaiisu; a grammar and dictionary with texts. (University of California publications in linguistics, v119) University of Calif. Press 1990 p393-9

Legal status, laws, etc.

Cole, Douglas, and Chaikin, Ira. An iron hand upon the people; the law against the potlatch on the Northwest Coast. University of Wash. Press 1990 p213-23

Legends

Echlin, Kim. Bibliography of Canadian Indian mythology. (Abhandlungen, no59) Völkerkundliche Arbeitsgemeinschaft (Germany) 1988 48p

Messer, R. A structuralist's view of an Indian creation myth. *Anthropologica* 31 no2:231-5 '89

Miller, J. An overview of Northwest Coast mythology. *Northwest Anthropol Res Notes* 23:134-41 Fall '89

Northern tales; traditional stories of Eskimo and Indian peoples; selected and edited by Howard Norman. Pantheon Bks. 1990 p335-43

Medicine

Garro, L. C. Continuity and change: the interpretation of illness in an Anishinaabe (Ojibway) community. *Cult Med Psychiatr* 14:450-4 D '90

Missions

Barker, J. Bibliography of missionary activities and religious change in Northwest Coast societies. *Northwest Anthropol Res Notes* 22:13-57 Spr '88

Mortuary customs

Logan, B. The Richland Crematorium; new evidence of plains woodland mortuary practices in the Central Plains. *Plains Anthropol* 35:122-4 My '90

Mythology

See Indians of North America—Religion and mythology

Newspapers

American Indian resource materials in the Western History Collections, University of Oklahoma; edited by Donald L. DeWitt. University of Okla. Press 1990 p171-236

Oratory

Haa tuwunáagu yís, for healing our spirit; Tlingit oratory; edited by Nora Marks Dauenhauer and Richard Dauenhauer; [pub. in assn. with] Sealaska Heritage Foundation. (Classics of Tlingit oral literature, v2) University of Wash. Press 1990 p559-69

Periodicals

American Indian resource materials in the Western History Collections, University of Oklahoma; edited by Donald L. DeWitt. University of Okla. Press 1990 p171-236

Psychology

Heinrich, R. K. and others. Counseling native Americans. *J Couns Dev* 69:132-3 N/D '90

Religion and mythology

Echlin, Kim. Bibliography of Canadian Indian mythology. (Abhandlungen, no59) Völkerkundliche Arbeitsgemeinschaft (Germany) 1988 48p

Haa tuwunáagu yís, for healing our spirit; Tlingit oratory; edited by Nora Marks Dauenhauer and Richard Dauenhauer; [pub. in assn. with] Sealaska Heritage Foundation. (Classics of Tlingit oral literature, v2) University of Wash. Press 1990 p559-69

Loftin, John D. Religion and Hopi life in the twentieth century. Indiana Univ. Press 1991 p144-63

Rites and ceremonies

Cole, Douglas, and Chaikin, Ira. An iron hand upon the people; the law against the potlatch on the Northwest Coast. University of Wash. Press 1990 p213-23

Haa tuwunáagu yís, for healing our spirit; Tlingit oratory; edited by Nora Marks Dauenhauer and Richard Dauenhauer; [pub. in assn. with] Sealaska Heritage Foundation. (Classics of Tlingit oral literature, v2) University of Wash. Press 1990 p559-69

Schleiser, K. Rethinking the Midewiwin and the Plains ceremonial called the Sun Dance. *Plains Anthropol* 35:24-7 F '90

Social life and customs

Hantman, J. L. Between Powhatan and Quirank: reconstructing Monacan culture and history in the context of Jamestown. *Am Anthropol* 92:686-90 S '90

Loftin, John D. Religion and Hopi life in the twentieth century. Indiana Univ. Press 1991 p144-63

Sources

American Indian resource materials in the Western History Collections, University of Oklahoma; edited by Donald L. DeWitt. University of Okla. Press 1990 p11-85

Annotated Bibliographies

Certain bibliographies are annotated—that is, they describe the books included. Some of these are lists of reference works with annotations. All libraries have bibliographies of this type and it is essential to consult them to find the best reference books on a subject.

The *Guide to Reference Books,* edited by Eugene P. Sheehy (10th edition, 1986), is an excellent example and is available in all libraries. Students will find it useful to read the few introductory pages in the front of the volume. Other similar guides are available; some are general, like the *Guide to Reference Books,* and others cover only specific subjects such as astronomy or American history. A few of these guides have been published in inexpensive paperback and would be a useful edition to any student's personal library. See the list after this chapter for additional examples.

After looking at the examples in Figures 5.1 and 5.2 and completing the exercises after this chapter the student will have discovered that there are many different formats for bibliographies. When preparing a bibliography of one's own for an assignment, a specific format may be desired. The sensible way to decide the appropriate format is to ask the teacher if he or she has any preference. Most formats include the information in generally the same order shown here, but punctuation and spacing and other details differ.

Author (last name first). *Title,* edition number. Place of Publication: Name of Publisher, date of publication.

The most important thing to remember is to be consistent, using the same order, punctuation and spacing throughout the bibliography.

Listed below are some popular term paper guides and style sheets. They all give instruction for, and examples of, bibliographic format. Additionally these guides provide invaluable information to the term paper writer, and all students should own one.

Term Paper Guides (see also Chapter 16)

The Chicago Manual of Style, 13th ed. Chicago: University of Chicago Press, 1982.

Fleischer, Eugene B. *A Style Manual for Citing Microfilm and Non-Print Media.* Chicago: American Library Association, 1978.

MLA Handbook for Writers of Research Papers, Theses and Dissertations, 3rd ed. Edited by Joseph Gibaldi and Walter S. Achtert, New York: Modern Language Association, 1989.

Thurston, Marjorie H., and Eugene S. Wright. *The Preparation of Term Papers and Reports,* 6th ed. Minneapolis: Burgess Publishing Company, 1970.

Turabian, Kate L. *Student Guide for Writing College Papers,* 5th ed. Chicago: University of Chicago Press, 1986.

VanLeunen, Mary-Claire. *A Handbook for Scholars.* New York: Alfred A. Knopf, 1978.

Exercises for Chapter 5

1. Find the bibliographies in your library for the two authors listed below. Answer the questions about both authors. If you have problems using the catalog or locating the books on the shelves, ask the librarian.
   (A) William Faulkner (see the subject card FAULKNER, WILLIAM 1897–1962 – BIBLIOGRAPHY):
       1. How many bibliographies does your library have on Faulkner?
       2. In what section of the library are the bibliographies located?
       3. Are the bibliographies of works *about* Faulkner, of works *by* Faulkner, or both?
       4. Do any of these bibliographies circulate?
   (B) Ernest Hemingway (See subject card HEMINGWAY, ERNEST, 1899–1961 – BIBLIOGRAPHY):
       1. How many bibliographies does your library have on Hemingway?
       2. In what section of the library are the bibliographies located?
       3. Are the bibliographies of works *about* Hemingway, of works by Hemingway, or both?
       4. Do any of these bibliographies circulate?
2. Read the preface to BIP, CBI and *LC Cat.*
   (A) Using the **author** section of BIP:

1. Count and record the number of entries for Stephen King.
2. What information is provided about each book?

(B) Using CBI for 1989:

1. Count and record the number of entries for Stephen King.
2. What information is provided in each entry?
3. Does this information differ from BIP? If so, how?

(C) Using NUC (**authors**), check the 1973–1977 accumulation for Stephen King.

1. Count and record the number of entries.
2. Check annual volumes or microfiche edition, if available.
3. How do the entries differ from those in CBI and BIP?

3. The following questions are based on Winston Churchill as a subject.

(A) Using the *Subject Guide to Books in Print,* count and record the number of entries.

(B) Using the last five years of CBI, count and record the number of entries.

(C) Under what heading(s) would you look for information about Winston Churchill in a guide to reference books?

(D) Check *LC Books-Subjects* for 1970 to 1974, and record the headings and subheadings providing information about Winston Churchill.

(E) Which of the sources checked provided the best information?

Important Terms in Chapter 5

BIP	*Books-Subjects*
NUC	LC Cat
CBI	*Bibliography of Bibliographies*

This chapter has described only a few bibliographies that can be useful in identifying materials not located by using the catalog. The following list include these plus a few more. Libraries will have many more bibliographies that those listed below. They may be found by using the subject approach to the catalog and by asking the reference librarian.

Important Books for Chapter 5

American Reference Books Annual, 1970– , ed. by Bohdan S. Wynar. Littleton, CO: Libraries Unlimited, 1970– .

Besterman, Theodore. *A World Bibliography of Bibliographies and of Bibliographical Catalogues, Calendars, Abstracts, Digests, Indexes and the Like.* 4th ed., revised and greatly enlarged. Lausanne, Switzerland: Societas Bibliographica, 1965–1966. 5 vols.

Bibliographic Index: A Cumulative Bibliography of Bibliographies, 1937– . New York: H. W. Wilson, 1938– .

Books in Print: An Author-Title Series Index to the "Publishers' Trade List Annual," 1948– . New York: R. R. Bowker, 1948– .

British Museum. Department of Printed Books. *General Catalogue of Printed Books.* Photolithographic edition to 1955. London: Trustees of the British Museum, 1959–66. 263 vols. (Supplements, 1956–1965, 1966–1970, 1971–1975, 1976–1985, 1986–1987, 1988–1989.)

Cumulative Book Index. New York: H. W. Wilson. 1928– .

National Union Catalog: A Cumulative Author List Representing Library of Congress Printed Cards and Titles Reported by Other American Libraries, 1953–1957. Ann Arbor, MI: Edwards, 1958. 28 vols. (5 year accumulations from 1958–1977.)

National Union Catalog, Pre-1956 Imprints: A Cumulative Author List Representing Library of Congress Printed Cards and Titles Reported by Other American Libraries. London: Mansell, 1968– . (610 vols.)

Sheehy, Eugene, comp. *Guide to Reference Books,* 10th ed. Chicago: American Library Association, 1986.

Subject Guide to Books in Print: An Index to the "Publishers' Trade List Annual," 1957– . New York: R. R. Bowker, 1957– .

United States. Library of Congress. *A Catalog of Books Represented by Library of Congress Printed Cards, Issued to July 31, 1942.* Ann Arbor, MI: Edwards, 1942–1946. 167 vols. (Supplements cover years 1942–1952.)

Walford, Albert John. *Walford's Guide to Reference Materials,* 5th ed. London: Library Association, 1980– . (Vol. 1, 1989, v. 2 1989, v. 3 1991.)

6. Book Reviews and the Parts of a Book

Objectives

After studying this chapter the student shall be able to
- find book reviews using available sources
- identify and use the different parts of a book

Book Reviews

After compiling a list of books on a topic, students may want to choose only several relevant ones for the term paper or other project. There are many types of book review sources and not all libraries will have all the sources.

Most books are reviewed in newspapers and periodicals. The trick is to find the appropriate review for a specific book. Some professional journals contain no articles, just book reviews. Some examples of these are *Choice, New York Review of Books,* and *Booklist.* Other journals, such as *Library Journal* and *Publishers Weekly,* include many reviews as well as articles covering many topics. Specialized periodicals such as *Journal of American History* review books only in that specialty.

Newspapers often include book reviews. The *New York Times* is the most useful source of newspaper book reviews. It includes book reviews in its daily paper besides the Book Review Section of the

Sunday edition. Reviews appearing in the *New York Times* may be located by using the *New York Times Index* under the subject heading book reviews. There is a list of the books reviewed arranged alphabetically by the author's last name. Anthologies—collections of works by many authors, usually poems or short stories—are reviewed and listed alphabetically by the title and found after the author list. The *New York Times Index* shows the date of the review, then page number of the edition and the column number of that page. Roman numerals or letters identify the section number of the edition. A typical listing follows:

Ja	6	III (or B)	19:	3
[month:	[day]	[section]	[page]	[column]
January]				

The most efficient process for finding book reviews is to use the indexes to periodicals. Some of these indexes specialize in book reviews, for example; *Book Review Index, Index to Book Reviews in the Humanities, Book Review Index to Social Science Periodicals* and *Current Book Review Citations.* Most libraries own at least one of the above titles. These indexes list the source of the book review, title of the periodical, volume number, date and pages. Figure 6.1 from *Book Review Index* is a list of reviews. Seventeen books by Dick King-Smith are listed and one to five reviews arc included for each title. The titles of the journals containing the reviews are abbreviated and the student must check the abbreviations list at the front of the volume to get the full title of each journal. Another useful source is *Book Review Digest,* which began publishing in 1905 and is issued monthly with annual accumulations. The *Book Review Digest* includes excerpts from reviews besides listing the location of the reviews in journals. It also includes the number of words in the review—which can be a vital clue to its scope (see Figure 6.2). The introductory page to *Book Review Digest* informs how selections for inclusions are made. To find reviews in professional or specialized journals it is necessary to consult the periodicals indexes for that field. For further discussion of periodical indexes see chapters 8 and 9.

To locate a book review use the index for the year the book was originally written, not a reprint date. If the review is not located in that year, check the following year, as reviews will appear up to a year or more after the publication date. Not all sources of book reviews

Figure 6.1. Book Review Index

King Horn - *King Horn (Allen)*
    Specu - v65 - Jl '90 - p564
King-Smith, Dick - *Ace: The Very Important Pig
(Illus. by Lynette Hemmant)*
    c   HB - v66 - S '90 - p602
    c   KR - v58 - Jl 15 '90 - p1004
    c   PW - v237 - Je 29 '90 - p102
*Alice and Flower and Foxianna (Illus. by John
Sharp)*
    c   GP - v28 - S '89 - p5229
Babe: The Gallant Pig (Iilus. by Mary Rayner)
    c   BL - v86 - N 1 '89 - p564
Beware of the Bull! (Illus. by John Sharp)
    c   GP - v28 - S '89 - p5229
Dodos Are Forever (Illus. by David Parkins)
    c   BFYC - v25 - Spring '90 - p21
    c   JB - v53 - D '89 - p279
    c   Sch Lib - v38 - F '90 - p19
E.S.P.
    c   Bks for Keeps - S '89 - p9
The Fox Busters
    c   GP - v29 - My '90 - p5356
The Fox Busters. Audio Version
    c   BW - v20 - Je 24 '90 - p8
Friends and Brothers
    c   Bks for Keeps - My '90 - p13

The Hodgeheg. Audio Version
    c   TES - D 22 '89 - p26
The Jenius (Illus. by Peter Firmin)
    c   KR - v58 - Je 15 '90 - p877
    c   SLJ - v36 - S '90 - p206
Martin's Mice (Illus. by Jez Alborough)
    c   Par - v64 - D '89 - p229
Martin's Mice. Audio Version
    c   Sch Lib - v38 - My '90 - p64
Sophie's Snail (Illus. by Claire Minter-Kemp)
    c   CBRS - v18 - Mr '90 - p90
    c   CCB-B - v43 - Ja '90 - p112
    c   HB - v66 - Ja '90 - p89
    c   HB Guide - v1 - Jl '89 p66
    c   SLJ - v35 - D '89 - p83
The Toby Man (Illus. by Ian Newsham)
    c   JB - v54 - F '90 - p27
*The Trouble with Edward (Illus. by Jacqui
Thomas)*
    c   GP - v28 - N '89 - p5245
    c   TES - F 2 '90 - p76
Kingdon, Jonathan - *Island Africa*
    Nature - v345 - My 24 '90 - p303
    New Sci - v127 - S 22 '90 - p66
    TLS - Je 29 '90 - p707

include all books and it may be necessary to consult several sources before locating a review.

Parts of a Book

Most books consist of a title page, preface, introduction, text and appendixes. Each of these parts contains useful information. Knowing where to find this information is helpful.

The title page (usually the first page with printing) gives the following information: (a) title of the book, (b) author(s), (c) publishing company, (d) place of publication, and sometimes (e) the date of publication. The back (or "verso") of the title page also contains useful information. It usually includes a copyright notice (name of the owner and a date frequently with the symbol ©) and sometimes edition and printing information (e.g., 2nd edition, 3rd printing; no such statement usually means it is a first edition). Recently publishers have also included cataloging information including subject headings. The ISBN (International Standard Book Number) identifies the publisher in a prefix (this publisher's is 0-89950-) and the actual book is the digits following (e.g.,

Figure 6.2. Book Review Digest

LAMBERT, DAVID, 1932—*Continued*
"The professional editing and evenhanded treatment of controversy come from one author, 18 advisers. and the Diagram Group production team. Text or diagrams are occasionally oversimplified, and there are two gross errors: oxygen does not 'burn carbon in the blood', and ooliths are not dinosaur eggs. . . . Otherwise, [this] is an impressively up to date and complete revision of Lambert's [A Field] Guide to Dinosaurs [BRD 1984]. The reading list contains all the right books but pulls punches in its comments, and is cluttered with obsolete popular works as well as technical material. . . . All this extraneous material, as well as the entire A-Z listing, can only have been shovelled in for the sake of doing so, never mind any relevance for the average reader. . . . Nevertheless, Dinosaur Data Book is excellent value as a good one-volume source on dinosaurs, if you can do without colour illustrations."
New Sci 128:56 O 27 '90. Michael Taylor (500w)

Sci Am 263:135 D '90. Philip Morrison; Phylis Morrison (130w)

"This is a well written, superbly illustrated, and thoroughly comprehensive book. . . . Almost every question that middle school-aged children through adults would ask about dinosaurs is answered. The line drawings and illustrations are all accompanied by a. diagram of a mouse, cat, dog. or human to which the reader can immediately compare the size of the dinosaur. Dinosaurs have attracted the attention of more humans than any other ancient species, and this comprehensive, yet succinct, overview will make their study even more enjoyable."
Sci Books Films 26:127 N/D '90. Hans O. Andersen (210w)

LAMBERT, GAVIN. Norma Shearer; a life. 381p il $24.95 1990 Knopf
B or 92 1. Motion picture industry 2. Shearer, Norma, 1900-1983
ISBN 0-394-55158-3   LC 89-43364

This is a biography of the actor who appeared in such movies as Marie Antoinette, The Women and Idiot's Delight. Index.

"[This book] is as much about the old studio days as it is about the widow of MGM's renowned Irving Thalberg. Though he never fully explains Shearer's apotheosis in Hollywood heaven, Lambert—a novelist and screenwriter with a deep romantic sense and a movingly elegant style—pegs her as proof of what the old system could do when it was fully cranked up. . . . Lambert cuts cleanly through the hype, while also acknowledging it. He has written a valuable book about the star system that happens, almost incidentally, to focus on one of its most successful products."
Christ Sci Monit p10 Ag 3 '90. Nat Segaloff (700w)

Libr J 115:117 Ap 1 '90. John Smothers (130w)

London Rev Books 12:20 S 13 '90. Gavin Millar (1100w)

LANDESMAN, CHARLES. Color and consciousness; an essay in metaphysics. 135p $24.95 1989 Temple Univ. Press
111   1. Knowledge, Theory of 2. Metaphysics 3. Consciousness 4. Color
ISBN 0-87722-616-4   LC 88-29442

The author "aims to support color skepticism—the view that nothing exemplifies or has any color. He . . . discusses various accounts of the nature of color, but he give special attention to three viewpoints: (1) that secondary qualities such as colors are dispositional properties of bodies, (2) that colors are physical microstates of bodies. and (3) that colors reside in consciousness. Landesman rejects the view that an adequate theory must preserve commonsense beliefs about colors." (Choice) Index.

"[The author] appeals to some evidence from empirical science supporting the notion that causal explanations of visual experiences in animals do not commit one to the existence of colored objects. In this respect, Landesman endorses the priority of empirical science to common sense. Overall, the book is clear, concise, and nontechnical. It provides a good introduction to philosophical views on color."
Choice 27:815 Ja '90. P-K. Moser (210w)

"Landesman argues that colour is neither objective nor subjective, and hence that nothing is coloured. What his arguments must really show, however, is that it is something neither objective nor subjective which makes 'our ascriptions of secondary qualities . . . true', when they are. So the framework of subject and object is not the whole story, and what Landesman has shown is that colour scepticism is part of the price that must be paid for supposing that it is."
Times Lit Suppl p758 Jl 13 '90. Jonathan Westphal (800w)

LANDRY, TOM. Tom Landry; an autobiography; [by] Tom Landry, with Gregg Lewis. 302p col pl $18.95 1990 Zondervan; -HarperCollins Pubs.
B or 92 1. Landry, Tom 2. Dallas Cowboys (Football team)
ISBN 0-310-52910-7 (Zondervan)   LC 90-33913

This is an autobiography by the football coach of the Dallas Cowboys.

"Landry's autobiography is pretty straightforward. He tells of his boyhood and his high school football heroics in tiny Mission, Texas; of leaving the University of Texas to serve as a B-17 pilot during World War II; of returning to Texas and Texas football, and then going on to the NFL. . . . He tells of his discovery of God during the late 1950s, and of how ever since he has prioritized his life: (1) God; (2) family; (3) career. It is Landry's life from Landry's perspective and it comes across much like the television image we have of him standing on the Dallas sidelines all those years—stalwart, to-the-point and in control, yet just a trifle inscrutable and more than a trifle wooden."
Christ Sci Monit p15 S 26 '90. Charles Fountain (550w)

"Landry's autobiography perpetuates the image that has earned him the respect of so many people. . . . Although the Christian influence on Landry and his 'aww shucks' naiveté seem overemphasized, Landry shows his skill as a motivating speaker and his genuinely 'nice guy' personality. The book will serve more as a motivating tool or speaker's sourcebook than it does as a behind-the-scenes view of Landry and his Cowboys."
Libr J 115:116 Ag '90. Martin J. Hudacs (130w)

N Y Times Book Rev p5 Ag 5 '90. Roy Blount (480w)

LANGMAN, LARRY. Encyclopedia of American spy films; [by] Larry Langman [and] David Ebner. (Garland reference library of the humanities, v1187) 443p il $49.95 1990 Garland
016.79143 1. Motion pictures—Dictionaries
ISBN 0-8240-5533-0   LC 90-3577

This compilation treats some one-thousand films of the espionage or intrigue genre. The compilers have "included comedies and musicals that depict activities involving undercover agents, government operatives, or spies. . . . The guide is limited to films produced by American companies. . . . The alphabetically arranged entries for films range in length from one paragraph to several columns. Each entry provides the date of release; releasing company; director, screenwriter, and principal performers; and summary of the plot. . . . [Some of the] entries include brief critical and historical commentary. . . . [There are also] 77 topical and biographical articles . . . [and] approximately 70 black-and-white stills." (Booklist)

this book is 895-2). The ISBN number is used not only for ordering books from the publisher, but as a unique identifier of that book, that edition, etc., among a possible group of very similar titled books. The ISBN is also used as a search key in OPACs, OCLC and other databases.

Most nonfiction books have a preface where the author explains what the purpose of the book is and many include acknowledgments (thanks to certain people for providing permissions, being of help, etc.). Further, many books include an introduction that frequently includes instructions on using the book. This is particularly true of books with many charts and tables. The introduction also may provide background information that makes the text easier to understand or use. The introduction is not necessarily written by the author. Students too frequently ignore a book's introduction, which leads sometimes to confusion in interpreting or using information it provides.

The text is the main body of the work. The appendixes (often spelled "appendices") might include a bibliography, index, maps, charts, graphs, etc., which have been added after the text. Consulting the bibliography will lead to additional sources of information. Using the index will help find information in the text easily and quickly. Some books may have a detailed table of contents in the front of the book that supplements or replaces the index. Most books have some sort of table of contents for locating general categories.

Book Review Sources

Book Review Digest, 1905– . New York: H. W. Wilson, 1905– .

Book Review Index, 1965– . Detroit: Gale Research, 1965– .

Book Review Index to Social Science Periodicals. Ann Arbor, MI: Pierian Press, 1978– (contents begin with 1964).

Current Book Review Citation, 1976–1982. New York: H. W. Wilson, 1976–1982.

Index to Book Reviews in the Humanities, 1960– . Detroit: Phillip, Thompson, 1960– .

Exercises for Chapter 6

1. Look carefully at the title page, back of the title page, table of contents, and index of this book. Note how they are arranged and what information is included.
2. Select one of the books about Winston Churchill that you found in BIP or CBI (Chapter 5) and look for reviews in the book review sources in your library.

Important Terms in Chapter 6

anthologies   Choice
ISBN   digest
New York Times Index

7. General Information Sources

Objectives

After studying this chapter the student shall be able to
- distinguish among the various types of dictionaries and determine which is appropriate for a particular word
- use a variety of encyclopedias to research a topic
- list the subject dictionaries and encyclopedias in a particular subject field
- list the handbooks, yearbooks and directories available in a particular field and obtain information available from them
- look up specific information in almanacs and other sources
- find and use gazetteers and atlases

Occasionally students seek answers to specific questions or definitions for particular words. The resources that supply these answers are called *general information sources*. Students have probably used some or all references previously in school, although they didn't know how to use them efficiently. The following discussion concerns the more common sources of general information and some alternate sources.

General Dictionaries

The most commonly used reference book is the dictionary. Yet students are often unaware that there are different types of dictionaries devised for particular uses. For most purposes a standard abridged desk size dictionary such as *The American Heritage Dictionary* is satisfactory for finding definitions of words, spelling and pronunciation. However, the standard dictionary is abridged, that means that the editors have selected the more commonly used words in the language and omitted many that are uncommon. If the student cannot locate a particular word in the standard dictionary he should consult an unabridged dictionary such as *Webster's Third New International Dictionary of the English Language Unabridged.* This volume contains many of, but not all, the words in the language, including the archaic (out of date) words, slang words and acronyms (words formed by accumulating the first letters of each of several words). These volumes are huge and expensive and are thus unlikely to be found outside of the library. These dictionaries may include special sections in the back that may be useful. A gazetteer is an alphabetical listing of famous or not-so-famous place names. Some sections contain short biographies of famous persons, such as royalty or presidents of the United States. Others contain specialized information such as flags of the countries of the world, population counts and dates of important events. A brief perusal of the back of the dictionary takes only a minute or two, but will save time later. Before using any dictionary the student should consult the directions found in the front of the book to understand the format of definitions and special symbols used, particularly pronunciation symbols.

Special Dictionaries

Although consulting an abridged or unabridged dictionary may provide all the information that is necessary, other special dictionaries may be checked for additional or more specific information. Some of these specialized volumes are dictionaries of slang, abbreviations, rhyming (containing lists of words that rhyme, especially useful when writing poetry), synonyms (words with the same or similar meanings), antonyms (words that have opposite meaning) and acronyms.

Using dictionaries such as *A Dictionary of Modern English Usage* by Henry Fowler is an essential tool in writing. This dictionary deals with points of grammar, syntax, style, and proper use of words and their spelling and preferred pronunciation and punctuation. It also contains commonly used foreign words and their meanings. There is even a dictionary containing commonly mispronounced words and another with commonly misspelled words. There are many foreign language dictionaries translating words from one language to another as well as dictionaries of archaic languages such as Joseph T. Shipley's *Dictionary of Early English*. A thesaurus is a kind of dictionary that lists synonyms and related words for each entry word. A thesaurus is useful when you know the definition of a word and want another way of expressing it.

Subject Dictionaries

Dictionaries have been compiled for special subject fields. Often the meaning of words vary when they are found in different subject contexts. For example, the word "mutant" in general usage usually refers to some product of genetic failure; however, the biological meaning of mutant is "any abrupt change in genetic structure," good or bad. These subject dictionaries clarify such subtle differences in meaning. The subject dictionary is considered a secondary source when the standard dictionary does not provide subtle differences.

The definitions supplied in subject dictionaries are devised by experts in that field and may differ from field to field. Subject dictionaries provide a more detailed and specific contextual definition and may provide cross-references to other useful terms. To locate these special dictionaries the subject headings in the catalog should be used. The same rules for subject headings stated in Chapter 4 apply to subject dictionaries. Also the librarian may guide one to the proper heading.

Encyclopedias

Encyclopedias, like dictionaries, come in a variety of types. The most familiar type is the multi-volume general encyclopedia, such as the *Americana, Britannica* or *World Book*. There are also multi-volume encyclopedias in foreign languages, such as *Encyclopedia Universalis,* (French), and *Gran Enciclopedia Rialp* (Spanish). Subject encyclopedias in both single volume and multi-volume sets are available. These subject encyclopedias are a valuable source of specific information. They include more detailed explanations than the ones given in general encyclopedias.

Examples of subject encyclopedias found in libraries are: *The Encyclopedia of Philosophy, The Catholic Encyclopedia, International Encyclopedia of the Social Sciences, Grove's Dictionary of Music and*

Musicians, Encyclopedia of World Art and *McGraw-Hill Encyclopedia of Science and Technology*. These are just a few examples of the hundreds of subject encyclopedias available. Most topical areas have encyclopedias associated with them.

The information in encyclopedias is updated, but not necessarily regularly. Information is added and deleted with new editions. The size of the article may change with new editions depending on new information and space available. Some articles go unchanged for ten years or longer. One must read the introductory statement in an encyclopedia to determine its policy on updating information and its frequency of publishing new editions. Some encyclopedias contain a manual to help in using that particular set. Finally, encyclopedias contain only summaries of important information and should not be considered the final word. One should keep in mind also that articles are usually written by individual experts and may contain opinions with which not every expert agrees.

Handbooks, Directories...

Everyone, at one time or another, needs some bit of information and thinks, "There must be a quick way to find this." There are many reference books that provide specific short answers and facts. Handbooks instruct on how to find and use this information. Handbooks are available on all subjects. It is vital to become familiar with the ones in a major field of interest and students may even wish to purchase one in their chosen field. The *Library Research Guide to Nursing* by Strauch contains information on the use of reference books and the major ones available, lists of indexes and available periodicals published in nursing. *The Handbook of Chemistry* contains graphs, tables and charts that are used frequently.

Yearbooks contain updated information in particular subject fields. These are extremely valuable, because besides periodicals, they contain the most current information available. *The Annual Review of Psychology* has summaries of selected topics with extensive bibliographies. These topics, however, vary from year to year. Such reviews are excellent starting points for researching topics for a paper since they are current and complete. A student or practitioner in a particular field would be well-advised to purchase or periodically read the annual reviews.

Most libraries have a collection of telephone directories from major metropolitan areas.

Almanacs are particularly handy in that they provide some unusually specific or obscure information. The *World Almanac* contains data such as the capitals of all the countries of the world, weights and measures used, the birth and death dates of famous persons, zip codes, addresses, population figures, records, and maps and so on. It is also an inexpensive purchase. Besides a dictionary, the almanac is a wise acquisition for the student. Although data are added or changed yearly, an almanac several years old is still valuable. Most libraries own several almanacs, which increases the probability that a particular item of information may be found.

Directories cover many subjects. Of course, the telephone book is a directory. Basically, all directories are lists of names, addresses and phone numbers. Some directories are annotated; that is, they include some explanation about the organization or corporation listed. See the list after this chapter for examples of directories. Information that may not appear in almanacs and encyclopedias may be found in statistical yearbooks and newspaper and periodical indexes.

If current events information is needed and the newspapers are unable to supply the needed information, try another current source such as *Keesing's Contemporary Archives, Congressional Quarterly Weekly Report* or *Facts on File*. Most libraries will have at least one of these sources.

Atlases and Gazetteers

There are many sources providing geographical information. Encyclopedias, almanacs and telephone directories all provide some geographical information and maps. Further, travel guides are valuable sources of information, including maps and textual information. Some travel guides are commercially produced hardcover books and others are inexpensive paperbacks produced by organizations such as the big oil companies (Mobil and Exxon travel guides, for example). Some organizations such as the American Automobile Association (AAA) also produce comprehensive travel guides. Commercially produced guides, of course, may be somewhat biased.

Commonly used sources of geographical information are atlases and gazeteers. Atlases contain maps and charts with all sorts of geographical information. Consult the map of the library you produced in Chapter 1 to locate atlases in the library. Besides a collection of maps, they frequently contain: 1. population data; 2. mileage charts; 3. statistics on imports and exports; 4. information on rainfall, agricultural and natural resources; 5. tourist attractions and national parks; and 6. photographs of cities and scenery. Gazetteers are lists of place names and people. A gazetteer is very helpful in locating places which have undergone a name change. Gazetteers may be separate volumes or appended to atlases.

Exercises for Chapter 7

1. Look up and record (briefly) the meaning of "memory" in the following:
   an unabridged dictionary
   an abridged dictionary
   any biological dictionary
   any social sciences dictionary
   any thesaurus

2. Look up and record the meaning(s) of "hip" in the following:
an unabridged dictionary
an abridged dictionary
any slang dictionary
any abbreviations dictionary
any acronyms dictionary
3. (A) Look up your home state or your hometown in two different encyclopedias (e.g., *Americana* and *World Book* and compare the entries.
   (B) Look up "strip mining" in two general encyclopedias and any subject encyclopedia you think may include an entry. Compare the articles and indicate the titles of the encyclopedias you checked.
4. List the subject dictionaries and encyclopedias in your major field of interest. Record the call numbers for future reference.
5. Locate on the shelves all the titles listed in question 4. Indicate which items circulate and which ones are multi-volume sets.
6. Take a term or concept in your major field of interest and look it up in a general encyclopedia and an encyclopedia in that subject. List the term or concept and briefly compare the articles.
7. Using the catalog, make a list of handbooks and guides in your library that deal with your major field of interest.
8. Locate in the catalog and on the shelves the almanacs and telephone directories. Do they circulate? If yes, explain briefly.
9. In general do yearbooks like *Statistical Abstracts of the United States* and the ones published by the United Nations circulate? Explain why or why not.
10. Using almanacs and statistical sources, look up your hometown or state and the college you attend (or one you know about).
    (A) How does this information on your hometown compare to what you found in the encyclopedia earlier?
    (B) Is the information about the college accurate?
    (C) Where else might you look for information about colleges?
11. (A) What kind of information does the telephone directory provide in the yellow pages?
    (B) Are zip codes in the phone book? If yes, where?
    (C) Are area codes listed in the phone book? If so, where?
    (D) What information about a community can be obtained by looking through the yellow pages?
12. Using the types of sources discussed in this chapter, answer the

following questions. List the sources checked and those which provided information useful in answering the question.

(A) Using three sources, find the address, zip code and phone number of McGraw-Hill, Inc., publishers.

(B) Using at least three sources, find the population of Denver, Colorado.

(C) Using five sources, list the population, geographical area and political leaders of Mexico.

13. Check the catalog and record the titles and call numbers of two gazetteers in your library.

14. Locate the atlases in your library, look through five, and record the types of information they contain in addition to maps.

Important Terms for Chapter 7

almanacs	directory
handbooks	atlas
yearbooks	gazetteer
unabridged	synonyms
abridged	antonyms
thesaurus	acronyms

Important Books for Chapter 7

Directories

American Art Directory, v. 1– , 1898– . New York: Bowker, 1899– . Every 3 years, 1952– . Addresses and information about art organizations, and traveling booking agencies.

Annual Directory of Environmental Information Sources, 1971– . Boston: National Foundation for Environmental Control, 1971– . Addresses of agencies and organizations, lists of books, documents reports, periodicals and films on the environment.

Darney, Bridgitte T., and Janice DeMaggio. *Subject Directory of Special Libraries*. 13th ed. Detroit: Gale Research Corp., 1989. (3 vols.)

Encyclopedia of Associations. Detroit: Gale Research, 1956– . Revised approximately every 2 years; 4 vol. Addresses and descriptions of organizations. Also lists defunct organizations.

National Faculty Directory, 1970– . Detroit: Gale Research, 1970– . Annual, 3 vols. Names and college or university affiliations of full-time teaching faculty. Schools not listed did not submit requested information.

New York State Industrial Directory, 1959– . New York: State Industrial Directories Corp., 1959– . Annual. Available for each of the 50 states. Names and addresses of industries including company officers, number of employees and products manufactured.

Towell, Julie, and Charles B. Montney. *Directories in Print.* Detroit: Gale Research, 1990. (Formerly *The Directory of Directories.*) An annotated classified list of directories with title and subject index.

Almanacs

Barone, Michael. *Almanac of American Politics.* Washington, D.C.: National Journal, 1972– . Annual. Arranged by state. Includes state and congressional districts, elected officials, campaign financing, congressional committees, etc.

Catholic Almanac. Huntington, IN: Our Sunday Visitor, Inc., 1969– . Annual. Catholic church organization, doctrine, history and brief descriptions of other religions, some statistics.

Information Please Almanac, Atlas and Yearbook, 1947– . Planned and supervised by Dan Golenpaul Associates. New York: Simon & Schuster, 1947– . Annual. Miscellaneous information, extensive historical and statistical information on the U.S., a general subject index and short biography section.

Japan Almanac. Tokyo: Mainichi Newspapers. In English, short articles on many aspects of Japanese history, culture and daily life, statistics and biographies, index.

The World Almanac and Book of Facts, 1868– . New York: World Telegram, 1868– . Annual. Now published by Pharos Books and distributed by St. Martin's Press. Up-to-date, reliable statistics; most comprehensive and most frequently used of all U.S. almanacs.

Encyclopedias

The Catholic Encyclopedia: An International Work of References on the Constitution, Doctrine, Discipline and History of the Catholic Church. New York: Catholic Encyclopedia Press, 1907–1922. 17 vols. Many long articles by experts. In addition to Catholic doctrine articles on general subjects such as literature and history. Somewhat out of date but still valuable. For newer information see the *New Catholic Encyclopedia* published by McGraw-Hill, 1967.

Encyclopedia of Bioethics. Warren T. Reich, ed. New York: Macmillan and the Free Press, 1978. 4 vols. Deals with many aspects of bioethics including such questions as abortion, euthanasia and the definition of death. Becoming dated.

Encyclopedia of Ethics. Lawrence C. Becker, ed. New York: Garland, 1992. 2 vols.

Encyclopedia of Psychology. Raymond J. Corsini, ed. New York: John Wiley & Sons, 1984. 4 vols. Contains biographies and short articles on theories, research and concepts in psychology.

Encyclopedia of Sociology. Edgar F. Borgatta, editor in chief. New York: Macmillan, 1992. 4 vols. Part of the update to the International Encyclopedia of the Social Sciences.

Encyclopedia of World Art. New York: McGraw-Hill, 1959–1968. Fifteen vols. plus two supplementary vols. Long articles with bibliographies. Approximately half of each volume is plates. All areas of art are included as well as all countries and periods.

International Encyclopedia of the Social Sciences. David L. Sill, ed. New York: Macmillan and the Free Press, 1968. 17 vols. Articles deal with all aspects of the social sciences, many cross references are included, some biographies and a good index. Updates have been issued as encyclopedias in various areas such as criminal law, justice, Third World, etc. Most of these are 2–4 volumes.

McGraw-Hill Encyclopedia of Science and Technology. An international reference work, 7th ed. New York: McGraw-Hill, 1992. 20 vols. Covers all branches of science except medicine and the behavioral sciences. Index volume. The set is kept updated with annual yearbooks.

Worldmark Encyclopedia of the Nations, 7th ed. Moshe Y. Sachs, ed. New York: John Wiley, 1988; distributed by Worldmark Press. 5 vols. Volume 1 is for U.N.; other volumes for Africa, Americas, Europe and Asia and Oceania.

Yearbooks

Demographic Yearbook/Annuaire Demographique, 1948– . New York: United Nations, 1948– . International demographic statistics from approximately 220 countries. This is one of a series of statistical yearbooks compiled by the United Nations.

Historic Documents of 19XX– . Washington, D.C.: Congressional Quarterly, Inc., 1972– . Annual. Chronological arrangement of speeches, letters, reports, etc., of importance. Cumulative index included in each volume. Detailed table of contents.

Statesman's Yearbook: A Statistical and Historical Account of the States of the World, 1864– . London, New York: Macmillan, 1864– . Not an almanac but brief and reliable descriptions, statistical information about countries of the world. Includes the countries' leaders, ambassadors and embassies and a bibliography of statistical information for each country.

United Nations. Statistical Office. *Yearbook of International Trade Statistics, 1950– .* New York: United Nations, 1951– . Annual. Provides annual trade statistics, imports and exports, many tables have comparative figures for several years.

United States Bureau of the Census. *Statistical Abstracts of the United States, 1878– .* Washington, D.C.: U.S. Gov. Printing Office, 1879– . Annual. Statistical summaries, most tables cover several years. First source to use national statistics. Leads users to other important statistical sources. Has useful supplements such as *County and City Data Book.*

Handbooks and Guides

Altman, Philip, and Dorothy S. Dittmer, eds. *Biology Data Book,* 2nd ed. Bethesda, MD: Federation of American Societies of Experimental Biology, 1972–1974. 3 vols. Tabular data for life sciences, includes some descriptive data. Each volume has a separate index.

Gibaldi, Joseph, and Walter S. Achtert. *MLA Handbook for Writers of Research Papers,* 2nd ed. New York: Modern Language Association of America, 1984. Widely used standards for preparation of articles, papers and books. This style information is also found in several term paper guides. See the bibliography at the end of Chapter 16.

Handbook of Chemistry and Physics. A ready reference book of chemical and physical data. Cleveland: Chemical Rubber, 1913– . 71st ed., 1990–1991.

Mullins, Carolyn J. *A Guide to Writing and Publishing in the Social Sciences.* New York: John Wiley, 1977. Guide to and information about writing papers, reports and articles for publication in the social sciences.

South American Handbook. A yearbook and guide to the countries and resources of South and Central America, Mexico and the West Indies, 1924– . London: Trade and Travel Pubs., 1924– . Descriptions of natural history, government travel and other information on the countries included.

Strauch, Katina, et al. *Library Research Guide to Nursing.* Ann Arbor, MI: Pierian Press, 1989. This is the latest in a series of library research guides from Pierian Press. They include information on selecting topics, organizing term papers, using the literature in the field (includes sample pages of reference sources), computerized literature searching and other aspects of library research.

Special Dictionaries

Aitchison, Jean. *International Thesaurus of Refugee Terminology.* Boston: M. Nijhoff, 1989.

Allen, Frederick Sturges. *Allen's Synonyms and Antonyms.* Rev. ed. Edited by T. H. Vail Motter. New York: Harper, 1938.

Bender, James Frederick. *NBC Handbook of Pronunciation,* 3rd ed., rev. by Thomas Lee Crowell, Jr. New York: Crowell, 1964.

Butress, F. A. *World Guide to Abbreviations of Organizations,* 8th ed., Detroit: Gale Research, 1987.

DeSola, Ralph. *Abbreviations Dictionary,* 6th ed. New York: Elsevier, 1981.

Fowler, Henry Watson. *Dictionary of Modern English Usage.* 2nd rev. ed. Edited by Sir Ernst Gowers. Oxford, England: Clarendon Press, 1965. Reprinted 1987.

Johnson, Burgess. *New Rhyming Dictionary and Poet's Handbook.* Rev. ed. New York: Harper, 1957.

Major, Clarence. *Dictionary of Afro-American Slang.* New York: International, 1970.

Oxford Dictionary of English Etymology, ed. by C. T. Onions with the assistance of C. W. S. Friedrichsen and R. W. Burchfield. Oxford, England: Clarendon Press, 1966.

Oxford English Dictionary, 2nd ed. Edited by J. A. Simpson and Edmund S. Weiner. Oxford, England: Oxford University Press, 1989. 20 vols.

Roget's International Thesaurus, 5th ed. Edited by Robert L. Chapman. New York: HarperCollins, 1992. New York: Crowell, 1977.

Shaw, Henry. *Punctuate It Right!* New York: Harper and Row, 1986.

Atlases and Gazetteers

Alexander, Gerald L. *Guide to Atlases: World, Regional, National, Thematic.* Metuchen, NJ: Scarecrow, 1971. An international listing of atlases published since 1950.

American Geographical Society of New York. Maps Department. *Index to Maps in Books and Periodicals.* Boston: G. K. Hall, 1969. 10 vols., supplements in 1971, 1976, 1987.

Barraclough, Geoffrey, ed. *The Times Atlas of World History,* 3rd rev. ed. Maplewood, NJ: Hammond, 1989.

Chambers World Gazetteer: A Geographical Dictionary. Edited by David Munro. New York: Cambridge University Press, 1990. Reprint of a 1988 edition with a slightly different title.

Cobb, David A. *Guide to U.S. Map Resources.* 2nd ed. Chicago: American Library Association, 1990.

Columbia Lippincott Gazetteer of the World. Ed. by Leon E. Seltzer with the Geographical Research Staff of Columbia University Press and with the cooperation of the American Geographical Society, with 1961 suppl. New York: Columbia University Press, 1962.

Goode's World Atlas. Edward B. Espenshade, Jr. Senior editor, Consultant Joel L. Morrison. 18th ed. Chicago: Rand McNally, 1990.

Kopal, Zdenek. *A New Photographic Atlas of the Moon.* New York: Taplinger, 1971.

NBC News Rand McNally World News Atlas, 1991. New York: Rand McNally, 1990. Published annually. Covers selected world events of the previous year.

Nelson, Theodora. *Good Books for the Curious Traveler: Europe.* Boulder, CO: Johnson Books, 1989.

Oxford Economic Atlas of the World. Prep. by the Cartographic Dept. of Clarendon Press, 4th ed. London: Oxford University Press, 1972.

Rand McNally and Co. *Rand McNally World Atlas.* Census ed. Chicago: Rand McNally, 1992.

Rand McNally Concise World Atlas. New York: Rand McNally, 1987.

Shepherd, William Robert. *Historical Atlas.* 9th ed. New York: Barnes & Noble, 1964. Reprinted 1980.

Special Libraries Association. Geography and Map Division. Directory Revision Committee. *Map Collections in the United States and Canada: A Directory,* 4th ed. New York: Special Libraries Association, 1985.

The Times. London. *The Times Atlas of the World: Comprehensive Edition.* 8th ed. London: Times Books, 1990. Considered the best atlas available.

U.S. Board on Geographical Names. *Gazetteer,* no. 130–142. Washington, DC: GOP, 1974–1977.

Webster's New Geographical Dictionary. Rev. ed. Springfield, MA: G. & C. Merriam, 1984.

Wright, George Ernest, and Floyd Vivian Filson. *The Westminster Historical Atlas to the Bible.* Rev. ed. Philadelphia: Westminster, 1956.

8. Periodicals and Newspapers

Objectives

After studying this chapter the student shall be able to
- identify the different types of periodicals and locate them in the library
- find specific information in periodicals
- distinguish between indexes and abstracts
- locate appropriate indexes and abstracts and use them to find information
- determine how to find periodicals at remote libraries
- find specific information in newspapers

Periodical Indexes

What is a periodical? What is a journal? What is a magazine? Students and teachers frequently use these terms. While there are slight differences in their meanings, for the purposes of this discussion these terms are identical and will be used interchangeably. They are publications that appear at regular, short intervals and contain articles, stories, poems, and essays about a specific subject, aimed at a specific age group, or at some other grouping determined by the editors.

For some students, the use of periodicals can be frustrating. They can't find anything pertinent in them. This is unfortunate because periodicals are vital in preparing most reports or term papers. The information in them is usually more current than the information in

Checking periodical indexes for citations.

books. Finding information in periodicals is not hopeless if the student uses the indexes to periodicals as tools.

Everyone has used an index of some sort, and most people are familiar with the indexes at the back of books. Everyone has used the yellow pages of a telephone directory, which is a type of index.

Individual periodicals may include an index for each volume or multi-volume indexes. Yet, these indexes are useful only if one knows which volume is needed. Unfortunately, this is not the typical situation. Therefore, *subject* indexes are more useful than *volume* indexes.

If students need the titles of journals published in a specific subject, they should consult a periodical directory. They are usually arranged by subject or have a subject index. Libraries will have at least one of the following directories: *Magazines for Libraries, The Standard Periodical Directory* or *Ulrich's International Periodical Directory*. Directories of periodicals in broad subjects (e.g. science) are also available. To enable one to find information published in journals, many comprehensive indexes and abstracts are available and are grouped into four categories:

1. *general,* that includes all relevant journals
2. *subject,* that are topic specific
3. *current,* only those of the present year or past two years
4. *retrospective,* covering a specific period of years.

Many are published by the same company and are in the same format. Having learned to use the "Wilson index" format, one can use almost every other index. The major difference between indexes is in which periodicals are included. The formats are similar.

An entry in a Wilson index under a particular subject heading includes:

1. title of the article
2. author's name
3. title of the journal, frequently abbreviated
4. date, which may include day, month and year
5. volume number
6. issue number
7. pages (see Figure 8.1)

Various indexes may not provide the information in the same order but all the information will be included. Indexes are published weekly, biweekly, monthly, quarterly and semiannually.

Perhaps the best known index and the most used is the *Reader's Guide to Periodical Literature* (RGPL), H. W. Wilson, publisher. The *Reader's Guide* indexes approximately 220 periodicals of general interest (popular magazines) and contains magazines such as *Life, Sports Illustrated, Time* and *U.S. News.* The *Reader's Guide* is current and general. An example of a general, retrospective index is *Poole's Index to Periodical Literature* that covers the years 1802–1906. An example of a current and subject index is the *Business Periodicals Index,* which indexes approximately 300 journals in the fields of business and economics.

Abstracts

Annotated indexes, known as abstracts, include additional information. They include all the information found in the index citation plus a brief description or summary of the article. This enables the user to figure out the content of the article without reading it. This may save

Figure 8.1. General Science Index

Oceanography
  See also
  Artificial satellites—Oceanographic uses
  Coasts
  Computers—Oceanographic uses
  Hydrographic surveying
  Paleoceanography
  Sounding
  Underwater laboratories
      Charts, diagrams, etc.
  The United States Navy's role in navigation and charting.
  J. E. Koehr. il *Oceanus* 33:82-5+ Wint '90/'91
      History
  Naval oceanography: a look back. S. B. Nelson. il maps
  Oceanus 33:11-19 Wint '90/'91
      Study and teaching
  Project Marco Polo [high school students travel through
  Indonesia, learning geography, culture and science]
  K. S. Frisbee. il *Oceanus* 33:79-81 Wint '90/'91
  Trends in ocean science. E. O. Hartwig. *Oceanus* 33:96-100
  Wint '90/'91
Octanoic acid *See* Caprylic acid
Octopuses
  An octopus's garden: in the Bahamas, an isolated saltwater
  pond brimming with octopuses and brittle stars offers
  a glimpse of life in ancient seas. R. B. Aronson.
  il *Nat Hist* p30-7 F '91
Odocoileus hemionus *See* Deer
Odocoileus virginianus *See* Deer
Odors
    See also
    Flavor

Fires and fire protection
  Desert fires cast a shadow over Asia. F. Pearce. il map
  New Sci 129:30-1 Ja 12 '91
  Environmental impact of fires in Kuwait. R. D. Small.
  bibl il map *Nature* 350:11-12 Mr 7 '91
  Gulf war could mean largest ever oil spill. F. Pearce.
  New Sci 129:18 Ja 19 '91
  Up in flames: Kuwait's burning oil wells are a sad
  test of theories. J. Horgan. il *Sci Am* 264:17+ My
  '91
Oils and fats
    See also
    Fish oils
    Food—Oil and fat content
    Glycerides
    Milk—Fat content
    Vegetable oils and fats
  Methods for measuring changes in deep-fat frying oils.
  P. J. White. bibl il *Food Technol* 45:75-6+ F '91
  Microstructure of peanut (Arachis hypogaea L. cv.
  Florigiant) cotyledons after oil cooking. C. T. Young
  and W. E. Schadel. bibl il *J Food Sci* 56:76-9 Ja/F
  '91
  A new look at the chemistry and physics of deep-fat
  frying. M. M. Blumenthal. bibl il *Food Technol*
  45:68-71+ F '91
  Regulation of frying fats and oils. D. Firestone and
  others. bibl *Food Technol* 45:90-4 F '91
  Safety aspects of frying fats and oils. W. L. Clark and
  G. W. Serbia. bibl il *Food Technol* 45:84-6+ F '91
Oilseeds
    See also
    Peanuts

Figure 8.2. Psychological Abstracts

4155. **Hu, Jun-chen.** (Fudan U School of Management, Shanghai, China) **Hobbies of retired people in the People's Republic of China: A preliminary study.** *International Journal of Aging & Human Development*, 1990, Vol 31(1), 31–44. —Analyzed hobbies of 551 retired individuals (aged 50+ yrs) in China. Data obtained through questionnaires were compared with responses of 100 younger people (aged 20–39 yrs). Hobbies of retired Ss were classified into 5 categories: reading, physical exercise, productive, visual-auditory, and recreational. There were significant differences between the hobbies of retired and younger Ss. Reading was most preferred by retired Ss. Gender, age, education, and previous occupation most influenced retired Ss' choice of hobbies.

4156. **Joebgen, Alicia M. & Richards, Maryse H.** (Loyola U, Chicago, IL) **Maternal education and employment: Mediating maternal and adolescent emotional adjustment.** Special Issue: Parent work and early adolescent development. *Journal of Early Adolescence*, 1990(Aug), Vol 10(3), 329–343. —52 mothers and their adolescent children (mean age 11.6 yrs), who were signaled by electronic pagers 7 times daily for 1 wk, responded by describing their actual and internal state at the time. At the end of the week, they also completed the Beck Depression Inventory, the Rosenberg Self-Esteem Scale, and a self-report measure of affect. When mothers were highly educated and employed or had less education and were unemployed and experienced high affect, their children also experienced higher daily affect, as well as

Figure 8.3. Abstracts of English Studies

UNITED STATES IV. THEMES AND TYPES

Biography

88-2007. Krupat, Arnold. *American Autobiography: The Western Tradition*, GaR, 35, 2, 1981, 307-17. One cannot speak of American Autobiography without including repressed types of American writing. The idea of American autobiography has been the Eastern version which is old-world oriented and self-consciously literary (from Benjamin Franklin to Gertrude Stein). Western American autobiography is much different: Daniel Boone, Davey Crockett, Jim Beckwourth, Buffalo Bill Cody, and even Mark Twain wrote from a non-cultured world, associated with Native American Indians, using oral traditions with an epic style hero moving through a comic structure (e.g. a happy ending). Often the autobiography had dual or confused authorship and was, in fact, committed to dominant social ideologies (sexism and racism) and was on the side of "white," though not cultured, civilization. N.H.

Children's Literature

88-2008. Shirley, Betsy B. *Visions of Santa Claus*, ABC, 7(ns), 12, 1986, 9-15. The eminent collector and dealer, A.S.W. Rosenbach, is also known as a scholar for his catalogue *Early American Children's Books*, 1682-1836. Though it would seem that he would be interested in Santa Claus, the annals of his life are silent on this topic. It is Mary Mapes Dodge who gives her version of Santa's biography in *St. Nicholas* (1975 issue), a children's magazine. To the Puritans, Santa was an unnecessary, if not evil, frivolity; he was only revived and given status in the 19th century when the Santa Claus story was enriched with the different customs of many nations, brought in by people emigrating to the US. A.I.D.

time, enabling the user to select articles to be read in a quick and easy way. Yet, these abstracts may not always be accurate; caution is the watchword when using abstracts. If the student is unsure, it is advisable to consult the article directly before discarding it or quoting it. *Psychological Abstracts* (Figure 8.2) and *Chemical Abstracts* are annotated indexes. These are the most useful tools in writing papers and theses. Abstracts may be prepared by the author of the article or by someone else who probably works for the publisher or abstracting service. To find the title of indexes or abstracts in a specific field in the library, look under the subject (in the catalog) and then look for the subheading indexes or abstracts. For example, chemistry — abstracts — periodicals.

Indexes and abstracts are generally arranged by subject, although some indexes interfile authors with subjects in one alphabet. Others have separate author index with cross-references back to the subject section. The abstracts are usually numbered (see figures 8.2 and 8.3). Most abstracts begin each volume with number 1. It is important to consult the proper volume. Figure 8.3 is a page from a monthly issue of

Abstracts of English Studies. Note that subject headings are in heavy black type with subheadings in the center of the column, the same technique used in Wilson indexes (see Figure 8.1). Each entry begins with:

1. the name of the author of the article
2. the journal title
3. volume number
4. date and pages

A summary of the article follows and the initials at the end are the initials of the person who wrote the abstract.

Some indexing/abstracting services also available in on-line or CD-ROM format also publish thesauruses of index terms. These thesauruses are as important to consult when searching the index or abstract as consulting LCSH when searching the catalog. Figure 9.1 on page 97 is from the thesaurus for *Psychological Abstracts/PsycINFO*. Note that it is similar to LCSH in providing B for Broader terms, N for narrower terms, R for related terms, UF and Use, etc.

Locating Journals

After the articles in the journals have been identified, the next step is to locate the journals in the library. Using the map constructed in Chapter 1 the location of the periodical stacks can be identified. These stacks usually contain the periodicals in alphabetical order. Each periodical may encompass several shelves. The indexes or abstracts provide the information needed about journal title, volume number, date and pages. The periodical's holdings list for the library is usually a circular or card file or may be a list printed by OCLC. This lists all the periodicals the library holds as well as the volumes owned. Journals for current months are usually located in a special section or reading area. Generally, periodicals do not circulate, since they are difficult or impossible to replace and are in high demand by library users.

Union List of Serials

What if the journal needed is not owned by the library? How can a library that owns the journal be identified? Union lists of serials show

Figure 8.4. Union List of Serials

commerce) Portland. v1-12 no3,S 10 1922-N
1931||
    1,1922-Ag 1923 as Oregon journal of com-
merce. v7 no8-v8 no7 omitted in numbering

CSt 3-[8-11]	OrCA
CU [4]-12	OrP 1-[10]
CtY [4]-12	OrPR [3]-[8]
	OrU 1[2]-[12]
IU 1-11	
NN 1[2]-[12]	WaS 6-[11]12

**OREGON business and investors, inc., Port-
land, Ore.**
Bulletin. *See* Your taxes

OREGON business review. (Oregon. University.
* School of business administration. Bureau
of business research) Eugene. 1,D 24 1941+

AU 1+	MCM 1+
AzU 1+	MH-BA 1+
C 1+	MdBJ 1+
CLSU 1+	
CSt 1+	
CU 1+	N 1+
CoU 1+	NBuU 1+
Ct 1+	NIC 1+
CtY 1+	NN 1+
DL 1+	NNC 1+
FU 1+	NNU 1+
IEN 1+	NcD 1+
IU 1+	NmU 1+
IaU 1+	OCl 1+
IdU 1+	OOxM 1+
In 2+	
InU 1+	OkU 1+
MBU 1+	OrCA 1+
OrP 1+	TxHR 4
OrPR 1+	UU [1]+
OrU 1+	VU 1+
PPT 1+	WU 1+
PU 1+	WaS 1+
RKS 1+	WaU 1+
RPB 1+	WyU 1+

OREGON cancer control news. Portland. 1,N
1916+

OrCA 2+	OrU-M 1+
OrP 1+	DNLM 1+

Figure 8.5. New Serial Titles

TITLE CHANGE
Equine business journal : EBJ. — Vol. 31, no. 10 (Oct.
    1990)-   — San Clemente, CA : Rich Publica-
    tions, 1990-
        v. : ill. ; 28 cm.
    Monthly.
    Title from cover.
    Continues: Western & English fashions.
    ISSN 1054-9323 = Equine business journal.
    1. Clothing trade—Periodicals. 2. Hat trade—Periodicals.
    3. Horse sports—Equipment and supplies—Periodicals.   I.
    Title: EBJ.
    WMLC L 83/9100   sf 90-92572
                  r687—dc12a˩
                                  AACR 2
    DLC

Equine veterinary education. — Vol. 1, no. 1 (Sept.
    1989)-   — Newmarket, Suffolk : R. & W.
    Publications, 1989-
        v. : ill. ; 29 cm.
    Quarterly.
    Title from cover.
    Established by British Equine Veterinary Association
    (BEVA).
    Other title: EVE
    ISSN 0957-7734.
    1. Veterinarians—Education—Periodicals. 2. Horses—
    Diseases—Periodicals. 3. Veterinary medicine—Periodi-
    cals. 4. Equine sports medicine—Periodicals. I. British
    Equine Veterinary Association. II. Title: EVE.
                           sn 90-16630
                            AACR 2
    CU-AM NIC PU ViBlbV

which libraries own which journals. They cover a range from local to international. The librarian may be consulted to locate the union lists. Libraries usually own the *Union List of Serial,* (ULS) third edition (Figure 8.4) and its supplements, *New Serials Titles* (Figure 8.5). The codes used to identify the holding libraries are the same ones that are used in the *National Union Catalog.* Figure 8.4 from the *Union List of Serials,* third edition is from the periodical *Oregon Business Review.* The entry states that the journal is published in Oregon by the University of Oregon School of Business Administration, and that it began publication in December 1941. The two columns of letters represent the libraries that own this periodical. The number following each letter code shows the volume number of the beginning volume in the holdings. For this journal most of the libraries' holdings begin with volume 1. The (+) after the volume number shows that the libraries own all volumes after volume 1. A key to the codes is found at the beginning of each volume of the *Union List of Serials*. The *New Serials Titles* (NST) format was the same as NUC (see Figure 8.5). A brief look at the organization of the code will help to identify many libraries without having to consult the list. Generally the code has three letters, the first, the state, the second the city and the third the name of the university. Some codes are one or two letters and some four. For example, NNC: N is "New York," thus the first N is for New York State, the second N is for "New York City," and the C is for "Columbia University." Likewise NNU is for "New York University," N for "New York State," N for "New York City" and U for "University." If the second letter is lowercase it is part of the state; CtY, Ct is Connecticut and Y is "Yale." Journal articles needed by students or faculty may be borrowed from other libraries (see Chapter 14 for interlibrary loans).

Newspapers

Although printed information has been available for thousands of years, newspapers as we know them did not develop until the early 17th century. Before then proclamations were read aloud to large crowds and were posted in the village square. Other ways of transmitting news (besides the town crier and troubadours or ballad singers) included news pamphlets and newsletters. A news pamphlet is usually a short small sheet of paper, folded once to make four pages, and is concerned with one subject. A broadsheet refers to a single sheet of large size paper frequently printed on only one side and posted as one might put up notices on a bulletin board. Broadsheets are also generally involved with one subject. Newsletters usually contain information supplied by one person but on many subjects. Newsletters have been common since the Roman times and are still an important source of information for the researcher. Many corporations produce specific newsletters on various topics. The Carnegie Foundation publishes a periodic newsletter with reports on current research financed by the trust. One should not overlook this source when researching a topic.

Early newspapers were printed sporadically at first, gradually becoming more frequent, once or twice weekly. Some earliest newspapers left one page blank for the reader or subscriber to add news before passing the newspaper to someone else. Church and government officials were quick to grasp the influence of newspapers, soon

Most libraries receive newspapers from major cities. Academic libraries may include foreign newspapers.

subjecting them to censorship, licensing, taxing and later bribery and prosecution of the editors, printers and writers (reporters). Copies of many early newspapers have survived and the newspapers of the last 350 to 400 years provide historical information, opinions of the times and other information not recorded elsewhere. Many early newspapers in Europe and in the United States invited writers to make unpaid contributions, thus becoming literary and political forums for the intellectuals. By the early 18th century, newspapers had become indispensable in politics and economics and continued to increase despite attempts by governments to control their number and content.

Newspapers in the 20th century have declined in numbers but individual papers have larger circulations. As costs increase, technology for production has become necessary for newspapers to survive. Most newspapers today are composed by computer and printed by photo-offset techniques developed since 1970. The new technology requires less staff and space for composing and printing.

Newspapers are read worldwide and are still a powerful influence on public opinion. They can build or destroy ideas, people or governments and range from the state-controlled propaganda sheets to the free press of the West. Debates about censorship continue. Western papers are expected to play a role in uncovering corruption and scandal, such as the role played by the newspapers in discovering the Watergate scandal. Modern newspapers provide services to researchers. Back issues are kept in a large collection, the "morgue," and are usually accessible to the consumer. Most newspapers also have a reference library that is used by the reporters and other staff preparing and editing articles. Large newspapers like the *New York Times* have comprehensive reference collections.

The type of information in newspapers falls into three general categories, (1) business and economic news, (2) governmental news, laws, politicians, elections and rulers and (3) social and neighborhood news. Newspapers are important sources of current information. Some are "newspapers of record" in that they print the full text of speeches, public notices and sometimes legislation. If the text of a speech by the governor of New York is needed it will be found in the *New York Times*.

Major newspapers are indexed. All important news and information in the *New York Times* is found by using the *New York Times Index*. The index lists the month, day, section number and page and column number. Other newspaper indexes use the same format. All contain subject entries and personal name entries with cross references. Be sure to check the abbreviations used and additional instructions at the beginning of the index. Library holdings of newspapers are generally on microfilm. For additional information see the section of Chapter 14 on nonprint materials. For additional information about newspapers check the catalog. For additional information about guides and directories, use subject headings guides (Chapter 2) or correct subject headings.

Exercises for Chapter 8

1. Check the card catalog for those subject headings pertinent to your major field of interest. List the indexes and abstracts in your library that relate to that field. If you do not find any listed in the catalog ask the reference librarian.
2. Check a guide to the literature in your major field of interest and record the titles of indexes and abstracts that are published but not available in your library. (Check *Guide to Reference Books* and other titles listed in Chapter 5.)

3. Check the catalog under the heading Periodicals — Directories; list the directories in your library with their call numbers.
4. Using the *Reader's Guide to Periodical Literature* (RGPL), v. 49, 1989 or v. 50, 1900, v. 44, 1984-1985, look up the subject Investment Fraud. Compare it to RGPL, v. 34, 1974-75 and v. 39, 1979-80 entries for Investment Fraud. Note subheadings and cross-referencing.
5. Using RGPL, recording the volume number and date, check the entries under the subject Iraq. Note the type of subheadings used and the "see" and "see also" references. Compare the entries for the years 1974-75 and 1990-91.
6. Check in the *Social Sciences Index, Business Periodicals Index* and *Education Index* under the subject heading Iraq. Record the title of index, volume number and year, type of subheadings and cross-references ("see" and "see also"). If your library does not have these indexes, check three other titles.
7. Look in the catalog for the subject card Periodicals. Record, with call numbers, those that may be useful, e.g. those listing periodical title abbreviations, bibliographies and indexes.

Important Terms in Chapter 8

Wilson Index	union lists
abstracts	newsletters
broadsheets	Reader's Guide
ULS	RGPL
NST	

Important Books for Chapter 8

Directories

Fry, Ronald W. *Magazines Career Directory: Guide to the Top U.S. and Canadian Magazine Publishers.* 4th rev. ed. Hawthorne, NJ: Career Press, 1990.

Katz, William Armstrong. *Magazines for Libraries: For the General Reader and School, Junior College and Public Library,* 6th cd. New York: R. R. Bowker, 1989.

Magazine Industry Market Place: The Directory of American Periodical Publishing. New York: R. R. Bowker, 1982.

Standard Periodical Directory, 1983–84, 13th ed. New York: Oxbridge Communications, 1990.

Ulrich's International Periodicals Directory. New York: R. R. Bowker, 1932– (yearly).

Indexes and Abstracts

Abstracts in Anthropology. Westport, CT: Greenwood, v. 1– , 1970– .

Abstracts of English Studies, 1958– . Boulder, CO: National Council of Teachers of English, 1958– (monthly).

Art Index. New York: H. W. Wilson, v. 1– , 1929– .

Bibliography and Index of Geology. Alexandria, VA: American Geological Institute, v. 32– , 1969– . Earlier volumes published under the title *Bibliography and Index of Geology Exclusive of North America.*

Business Periodicals Index, 1958– . New York: H. W. Wilson, 1958– (monthly).

Chemical Abstracts, 1907– . Columbus, OH: American Chemical Society, 1907– (weekly).

Cumulative Index to Nursing and Allied Health Literature. Glendale, CA: Glendale Adventist Medical Center, v. 1– , 1956– . Earlier volumes have a slightly different title.

General Science Index. New York: H. W. Wilson, v. 1– , 1978– .

Historical Abstracts. Santa Barbara, CA: ABC Clio. v. 1– , 1955– . Beginning with v. 17, 1971 it is published in four parts per volume.

Humanities Index. New York: H. W. Wilson, v. 1– , 1971– . Earlier title was *Social Sciences and Humanities Index,* preceded by the *International Index.*

Index to Government Periodicals, 1970– . Chicago: Infodata International, 1970– (quarterly, with annual circulation).

The Magazine Index, 1977– . Belmont, CA: Information Access Corp., 1977– .

MLA International Bibliography of Books and Articles on the Modern Languages and Literature. New York: Modern Language Association of America, 1921– .

Pooles's Index to Periodical Literature. Reprinted. Gloucester, MA: Peter Smith, 1963. (7 vols. covering 1802–1906.)

Psychological Abstracts, 1927– . Lancaster, PA: American Psychological Association, 1927– (monthly).

Reader's Guide to Periodical Literature, 1900– . New York: H. W. Wilson, 1900– (semi-monthly).

Recently Published Articles. Washington, DC: American Historical Review, v. 1– , 1976–1990. Formerly published as a section of the *American Historical Review.*

Social Science Citation Index. Philadelphia: Institute for Scientific Information, v. 1– , 1973– . The same publisher also issues *Science Citation Index* and *Arts and Humanities Citation Index.*

Social Sciences Index. New York: H. W. Wilson, v. 1– , 1974– . Earlier title was *Social Sciences and Humanities Index* which was preceded by *International Index.*

Sociological Abstracts. San Diego, CA: Sociological Abstracts, v. 1– , 1952– .

Newspaper Indexes

New York Times Index. New York: New York Times Co., 1913– . Earlier series index the *New York Times* from September 18, 1951.

Personal Name Index to the New York Times Index, 1851–1974. Succa-Sunna, NJ: Roxbury Data Interface, 1976. Supplements to main set have been issued to 1989.

The Times Index. Reading, England: Newspaper Archive Developments, 1973– . 1790–1905 indexes as *Palmer's Index to the Times Newspaper.* Indexes to other years published by various publishers.

Wall Street Journal Index. New York: Dow Jones, 1958– . Starting in 1981, the index includes *Barron's Index.*

Washington Post Index. Ann Arbor, MI: University Microfilms International, 1989– . Earlier volumes published by other publishers.

Union Lists

New Serials Titles. New York: R. R. Bowker. A union list of serials commencing publication after December 31, 1949. Sets for the years 1950–1970 (4 vols.), 1971–1975 (2 vols.), 1976–1980 (2 vols.), 1981–1985 (6 vols.), 1986–1989 (6 vols.), monthly, quarterly issues and annual volumes.

Union List of Serials in Libraries in the United States and Canada, 3d ed. New York: H. W. Wilson, 1965 (5 vols.).

Other Helpful Books

Alkire, Leland G., ed. *Periodical Title Abbreviations,* 7th ed. Detroit: Gale Research, 1989.

Kujoth, Jean Spealman. *Subject Guide to Periodical Indexes and Review Indexes.* Metuchen, NJ: Scarecrow, 1969.

9. CD-ROM Indexes and On-Line Database Searching

Objectives

After studying this chapter the student shall be able to
- distinguish between CD-ROM searching and On-Line Searching
- search a CD-ROM index
- construct a Boolean search

General Information

Periodical indexes are available on CD-ROM and through on-line database vendors besides the traditional paper format. These formats provide methods of finding information not available when using the paper format. It is possible to combine terms and do a customized search. CD-ROM indexes are available in many libraries. Each work station is usually devoted to only one index. The workstation is comprised of a mini-computer with a hard drive, one or more floppy drives and a CD player. New technology and networking may provide access to several indexes from one work station. Searches on CD-ROM indexes are very fast. The computer not only allows the combining of subject terms but also may allow keyword searching. In a keyword search the user instructs the computer to search for a word any place in the citation, not just the subject, author's name or first word of the title. Students must remember that all periodical citations from indexes in any format have equal importance or value. Further they should discriminate which citations to pursue. A major disadvantage of a CD-ROM work station is that only one person can use it at a time.

On-line searching of periodical indexes is available through commercial vendors. The user contacts these vendors via modem. They must establish an account with the vendor and pay for the services used.

CD-ROM databases usually have all the necessary instructions on the screen. Each vendor of on-line databases uses unique commands for searching. The student must learn the searching commands for that vendor's system and sometimes additional commands for a particular database in the system. Vendors charge for time connected to the system and for each item retrieved, either viewed or printed. On-line searching may be prohibitively expensive.

CD-ROM Products

There are many periodical indexes available in CD-ROM format. Some periodical indexes and other reference sources on CD-ROM may be available from several vendors. Vendors use different programs to get information from the CD-ROM. Fortunately, CD-ROM indexes supplied by the same vendor use the same software. Once the student masters the strategies and commands for a particular vendor, he may use any CD-ROM distributed by that vendor. Some vendors also use CD-ROM players that can hold more than one CD. This makes it easy to switch indexes without switching work stations. There are nearly 1,500 CD-ROM products listed in the 1991 edition of *CD-ROM in Print*.

InfoTrac

"InfoTrac" is the name of CD-ROM products from Information Access Corporation (IAC) of California. IAC has several indexes including *National Newspaper Index*, *Magazine Index*, *Academic Index*, and *Health Index*. Libraries that subscribe to more than one of IAC's CD-ROM indexes have separate work stations for each index or one work station with a sort of jukebox CD player called a tower. Using a tower the student may search several indexes from the same work station. The data on the CD is indexed using LCSH as its authority for subject headings. The latest citations appear first in the list of citations retrieved in a search. InfoTrac provides clear instructions at the bottom of the screen. These include searching, moving from one heading to another, starting a new search and moving from one citation to another.

IAC is continually improving its search software. In January 1991, IAC introduced software that included added search capabilities for an "expanded search." This allows the student to go from the current search to a Boolean search using *and*. The user does not type in *and* between words. The software assumes the *and* between words in an expanded search. Further it is possible to change the search without retyping. In 1992 additional features (EF—extended family) were added, such as EasyTrac (the general, simple search) and PowerTrac (which includes many advanced searching methods). The EasyTrac allows the searcher to choose between a subject and a keyword search. If the word is not found in the subject index, EasyTrac automatically does a keyword search. EasyTrac also includes options for limiting or defining the search. The help is context sensitive, describing the current situation. The Boolean *and, or* and *not* can be used with the new software. Truncation of terms is permitted although the use of parentheses is not allowed for nesting of terms. Truncation symbols of *, ? and ! are used. PowerTrac can be accessed by using Alt F10. PowerTrac allows many more ways of searching including the range operator *since, after, to,* and *before*. There are many options using the Alt key, which allows browsing keywords, spelling, review of past searches and inserting Boolean operators. Many pop up menus are included in the PowerTrac system.

Libraries may allow students to copy citations to their own disks instead of using the printer. This option will vary according to the InfoTrac work station, the number of floppy drives available and the library's policies. Some entries in the index include abstracts or full text of the article or report. In full text items, it is useful to be able to print to a disk to save paper.

Another excellent feature, available from some OPACs, is the system's inclusion of all the subject headings assigned to an article. The student then selects another subject heading from the screen. This subject heading is automatically searched and the citations appear on the screen. The user need not restart the search.

InfoTrac computer/CD-ROM is popular among students. Easy to follow directions are provided on the screen.

InfoTrac shows the number of pages in an article contained within parentheses after the number of the starting page; eg. 176(3). This means that the article begins on page 176 and is three pages long. It is possible that advertisements are interspersed within the text of the article. Thus beginning and ending page numbers might lead the student to believe that the article is longer than it is.

Subscriptions from InfoTrac are available for 9 months or 12 months. Those schools that do not hold summer classes have 9 month subscriptions and do not receive monthly updates during the summer.

IAC includes major news stories from the *New York Times* in its indexes. The coverage is usually the previous 6 months. The indexing included on IAC products is more current than the *New York Times Index* by about one month. There is one caution. IAC indexes the late edition and the national edition of the *New York Times*. If the *New York Times*' citation has an **L** it indexes the late edition, and **N** in the citation means the national edition was indexed. The microfilm is the late (**L**) edition. Articles might appear on a different page of the microfilm edition of the *New York Times* than students find in the InfoTrac citation. InfoTrac also indexes some news stories from the *Wall Street Journal*. **W** shows the Western edition and **E** the Eastern edition. The edition in the library matches parts of the country. Check with the librarian to see what edition your library receives.

WILSONDISC and WILSONLINE

These are CD-ROM versions of the Wilson indexes discussed in Chapter 8. As of January 1991 there were 20 Wilson indexes available in CD-ROM format. The CD versions contain indexes from 1982 to the present. Updates are issued quarterly. The menu allows the user to search recent information by using the WILSONLINE. WILSONLINE and WILSONSEARCH are available 24 hours a day, 7 days a week.

Libraries which subscribe to WILSONDISC receive unlimited searching on WILSONLINE without additional charges. WILSONLINE provides access to 26 databases (as of 1991) and can be a "pay as you go" system. The searcher or library is charged per search without charges for connect-time, royalties, etc., that are charged by other database vendors such as DIALOG, BRS, and LEXIS-NEXIS. WILSONSEARCH is a service allowing access to 19 databases for searchers without prior searching experience. The searcher is guided by a series of menus. Charges are per search, defined as 10 citations. No charges are incurred if no citations are found. Generally the software searches by author, title or subject, the same way the paper indexes are searched.

As in InfoTrac and many OPACs, the item searched is highlighted and the screen displays those entries immediately before and after the searched term. If the search contains no records, a function key searches related subjects or uses the WILSONLINE. Wilson indexes are now accessible via OCLC's EPIC and FirstSearch options. As of February 1993 there are 8 Wilson indexes available through EPIC and FirstSearch. The searching of the Wilson indexes via OCLC are done through OCLC's software and is different from Wilson's software. See Chapter 14 for more information on OCLC and its EPIC and FirstSearch systems.

SilverPlatter

The SilverPlatter Corporation issues many indexes in CD-ROM form. Among the titles available from SilverPlatter are PsycLIT, ERIC, and MEDLINE. Thesauruses are available for many of these indexes on CDs. These thesauruses are also helpful when searching these same indexes with an on-line system or in paper format (see Figure 9.1). Some products provided by SilverPlatter have a tutorial. If the library has SilverPlatter products, ask the librarian about the availability of a tutorial program. The software allows many more types of searches than Infotrac or WILSONDISC.

The Boolean search operators include *and, or, not, near, except, with.* There are many more choices than with most or all OPACs. Searching SilverPlatter products successfully requires training, while it is possible to search InfoTrac and WILSONLINE successfully with little or no instructions. Searching SilverPlatter products is similar to searching on-line databases. The student can employ the same search strategies and save money.

SilverPlatter allows the student to search for terms that appear in the database or in a specific field, e.g., author field or date field. Searches consist of two parts: 1. *finding* records and 2. *showing* records on the screen. After the student locates the record, they may opt for printing records or copying to a floppy disk. Some libraries may not permit downloading due to equipment constraints or library policy.

In SilverPlatter it is possible to combine two previous searches by combining the search set number connected by a Boolean operand. For example "find #3 and #4" combines the results of the 3rd and 4th searches, then displays those that contain terms that appear in both set 3 and 4. The screen display shows the search or set number under the *no.* heading. The next column shows the number of records containing the search term. A search for entries on apple trees might appear as:

no.	records	request
#1	10	Apple
#2	2000	tree
#3	5	Apple tree

The system assumes that the word *and* appears between two words typed next to each other. The above example shows that 10 records

Figure 9.1.
Thesaurus of Psychological Index Terms

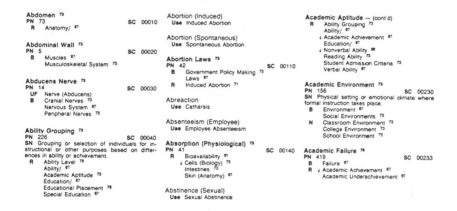

contained the word "apple" and 2000 contained the word "tree." Further, 5 records contained both words although the words may not be touching or even in the same field. If the search was continued the following would also appear on the screen:

| #4 | 6020 | Fruit |
| #5 | 700 | #2 AND #4 |

The search continues for the records containing the term *fruit*. Then it combines the searches for *fruit and* the search for the term *tree*. New searches are added to the screen until the system is restarted or a preset period elapses with no new entries added.

One may narrow a search using the word *and* to find two words or terms that appear in the same record. One widens a search by using *or*. *With* means that the terms must appear in the *same field* and thus the search will be more specific (narrower) than a search using *and*. The use of *near* with a number, e.g. *Apple NEAR 2 Tree* results in those records where apple and tree are in the same field. They will be within two (2) words of each other. The searches using *near* are narrower than those using *with*. SilverPlatter work stations may have one or more multiple CD drives. The arrangement of the CD drives determines the number of indexes the user can search from the same work station.

Database Summaries

The InfoTrac is easy and fast. The SilverPlatter's time to complete a search is also fast while WILSONDISC is the slowest. The SilverPlatter and InfoTrac systems provide all the citations in one list on the screen whereas WILSONDISC searches each time the student wants to see the next citation. SilverPlatter gives the most extensive search capabilities and thus gives citations for the most narrowly defined topics. InfoTrac's 1992 software updates allow more searching options by providing two levels, easy and complex. The PowerTrac comes close to SilverPlatter and on-line database searching in allowing the searcher to precisely define a search.

LANs — Local Area Networks

Libraries with CD-ROM indexes and OPACs and a LAN may install the CD-ROM indexes on a mainframe computer. The student may then reach any of the CD-ROM indexes from the same computer used to search the OPAC. Thus, several users can have access to the CD-ROM index simultaneously.

Searching Databases On-Line

The vendors used by most libraries are DIALOG and BRS. These vendors have hundreds of database files available. Both require users to have accounts for billing purposes. The charge for using each database may differ and is based on connect-time (charged by the minute or hour) and the number of citations that are printed. Charges for on-line and off-line printing may differ. Vendors supply brief instruction sheets for each database including search keys, formatting of records, information about database and charges. Manuals are revised periodically. Few libraries allow students to search these databases without prior training. The student and the librarian discuss the search and both are present during the search. Students should practice searching in print indexes before doing a database search. Individual databases have thesauruses to consult. Interaction between the librarian and the student during the search improves the efficiency of the search.

Some vendors group the databases into different groups to allow rapid access to all databases for a particular search. The searcher may use several databases at once. Some journals are indexed in more than one index. Requesting the system to check for duplicate citations and remove duplicates before printing the citations is cost efficient.

Some databases contain the full text of the article (or reference book) and the standard index citations. It is expensive to print the full text. The vendor's charges start at $9 and may be as much as $200 per item.

Exercises for Chapter 9

1. What CD-ROM products does your library subscribe to? Is there a printer attached?
2. Does your library provide on-line database searching? Who does the searching? Is there a charge?
3. Look up the subjects checked for other indexes. See exercises for Chapter 8. (Iraq, investment fraud, memory)

Important Terms for Chapter 9

WILSONDISC	Boolean
InfoTrac	vendor
WILSONLINE	work station
BRS	downloading
DIALOG	IAC
SilverPlatter	WILSONSEARCH

Important Books for Chapter 9

Database Directory. White Plains, NY: Knowledge Industry Publications, 1984– . Directory of "databases accessible online in North America."

Directory of Portable Databases. New York: Cuadra Elsvier, 1990– . Semiannual, v. 1, no. 1– . January 1990.

Frey, Donnalyn, and Rick Adams. !%@, *A Directory of Electronic Mail Addresses and Networks*. 2nd ed. rev. and updated. Sebastopol, CA: O'Reilly and Associates, 1990.

LaQuey, Tracy L. *The User's Directory of Computer Networks*. Bedford, MA: Digital Press, 1990.

Online Database Search Services Directory: A Reference and Referral Guide to Libraries, Information Firms and Other Sources Providing Computerized Information Retrieval and Associated Services Using Publically Available Online Databases. John Schmittroth, Jr., and Doris Morris Maxfield, eds. Detroit, MI: Gale Research, 1984- .

10. Literature and Criticism

Objectives

After studying this chapter the student shall be able to
- locate poems, short stories and other forms of literature published in anthologies and periodicals
- find critical analyses of plays, poems, short stories, novels and speeches
- identify and record the indexes of literary forms owned by the library
- locate plot summaries

General Information

Literary forms include plays, poems, short stories, novels and speeches. Obviously, there are many items that one might want to retrieve. Finding one poem may be difficult or impossible if one only uses the card catalog. Students will find the task less demanding if they consult a special catalog, anthology or index. Poems, short stories and essays are usually published in collections called anthologies or in subject-specific periodicals. Anthologies may include the works of one or multiple authors. The scope is determined by the editor. With practice the student will find anthologies by using the catalog. Correct subject headings are essential to seeking materials. The subject heading books (see Chapter 4) provide alternate headings useful in this task. For example, to locate a particular play, the correct heading is drama, not plays. With some practice one will learn key subject headings and no longer need to consult the book each time a subject heading is needed. Besides using anthologies, the student will use alternative research sources, such as indexes, catalogs and abstracts.

Indexes and Catalogs

The *Short Story Index* (Figure 10.1), published by the H. W. Wilson Company, is a guide to locating short stories that have been published in collections. The index lists the stories by author's name, title and subject, and all entries are in one alphabet. Also it identifies the book or periodical title in which the story appeared. For example, Goldman's story "Way to the Dump" is in the collection *Best Stories from New Writers* edited by L. Sanders. The format is typical "Wilson" format (see Chapter 8). This index is extremely comprehensive and should be sufficient for most purposes.

The *Essay and General Literature Index* is a guide to essays and short articles published in books rather than in periodicals. For information about an author, one looks under the author's name. There are also subject headings to provide access to items when the author's name is unknown to the student. Figure 10.2 is a typical entry. The author's name, Hemingway, heads the entry. In the center of the column, the term "about" shows that the items under this heading are articles about Ernest Hemingway—biographical information, but not written by him. The first item is by A. C. Bredahl, titled "Hemingway: the body as matrix" in a collection by A. C. Bredahl, *New Ground* on pp. 68–87. Further down the column the heading appears in the center, "About individual works." Under this heading are articles about *Garden of Eden, Hills Like White Elephants* and *The Sun Also Rises*. For complete information about anthologies indexed in *Essay and General Literature Index*, see the back of each volume.

Speeches and plays are indexed in respective volumes. *The Speech Index*, edited by Robert Sutton, has been enlarged several times and is comprehensive. The *Play Index*, another Wilson index, is arranged in the typical format with the plays arranged by subject, author and title in one alphabet. The entries include information such as the number of acts, the number of male and female roles, the number of scenes, and in which collection the plays appear.

The *Fiction Catalog* (Figure 10.3) is also published by Wilson. It is

Figure 10.1. Short Story Index

The glen. Jacobsen, J.
Glickman, James
  Homesick
    Ladies' Home Journal 106:80+ Jl '89
Glimmer, glimmer. Effinger, G. A.
A glorious Fourth. Faulk, J. H.
The glorious Pacific way. Hau'ofa, E.
GLOUCESTERSHIRE. (ENGLAND)   *See*
  England—Gloucestershire
Glover, Douglas H.
  Why I decide to kill myself and other jokes
  The Best American short stories, 1989
GLOVES
  Edgeworth, M. The limerick gloves
Go, lovely Rose. Bates, H. E.
GOATS
  MacLeod, C. Fifty acres of prime seaweed
GOD
  Donnelly, M. As a still small voice
  Spruill, S. G. Silver
The god and his man. Wolfe, G.

Goldman, E. S.
  Way to the dump
    Best stories from new writers; ed. by L.
    Sanders
Goldreich, Gloria
  Eight candles of hope
    McCall's 117:73-7 D '89
  The prayer shawl
    "The Safe deposit", and other stories
    about grandparents, old lovers, and
    crazy old men; ed. by K. M. Olitzky
Goldsmith, Oliver, 1728-1774
  Adventures of a strolling player
    The Oxford book of Irish short stories
Goldstein, Lisa
  Death is different
    The Year's best fantasy: second annual
    collection
  My year with the aliens
    Full spectrum [1]; ed. by L. Aronica and
    S. McCarthy

one of the few sources that provides an index to novels by subject. If a novel about the Revolutionary War is needed, a check of the *Fiction Catalog* would provide a list of novels by authors and titles about the Revolutionary War. The *Fiction Catalog* gives book reviews for many novels listed. There are additional catalogs to "fictions by special subjects," such as science fiction or mysteries.

Grangers Index to Poetry is a selective index to poems that appear in generally accessible collections. There are several editions that include many anthologies published over the years. A poem may be located by using the author index, the subject index, or the title or first line index. The preface of the *Poetry Index Annual* declares that it "has been developed to provide access to the preponderance of anthologized poetry which is not indexed anywhere." It also claims to be the "only work to systematically index *all* anthologies as they are published." The dictionary format provides entries by author, title and subject.

Criticism and Interpretation

Articles concerning literary works may be found by using the card catalog, periodical indexes and explicators. When using the catalog look for the subheadings Criticism and Interpretation. For example, Stevenson, Robert Louis 1859–1895 — Criticism and Interpretation.

Figure 10.2. Essay and General Literature Index

Hemingway, Ernest, 1899-1961
About
Bredahl, A. C. Hemingway: the body as matrix. (*In* Bredahl, A. C. New ground p68-87)
Ellmann, R. The Hemingway circle. (*In* Ellmann, R. A long the riverrun p199-203)
Godden, R. 'You've go to see it, feel it, smell it, hear it', buy it: Hemingway's commercial forms. (*In* Godden, R. Fictions of capital p39-77)
About individual works
Garden of Eden
Solomon, B. P. Ernest Hemingway's real Garden of Eden. (*In* Solomon, B. P. Horse-trading and ecstasy p22-31)
Hills like white elephants
Wilt, J. Abortion and the fear of the fathers: five male writers. (*In* Wilt, J. Abortion, choice, and contemporary fiction p101-31)
The sun also rises
Balassi, W. Hemingway's greatest iceberg: the composition of The sun also rises. (*In* Writing the American classics; ed. by J. Barbour and T. Quirk p125-55)
Phillips, K. J. Bowing to the bull. (*In* Phillips, K. J. Dying gods in twentieth-century fiction p65-81)
Bibliography
Brenner, G. Fitzgerald and Hemingway. (*In* American literary scholarship, 1988 p153-76)
Stark, B. Ernest Hemingway. (*In* Sixteen modern American authors; ed. by J. R. Bryer p404-79)

An explicator is a bibliography of articles about a literary work. Most explicators are specific, e.g. the poetry explication. There are guides, histories and dictionaries available for forms of literature. Concordances are also available for many authors and for specific works, such as the Bible. A concordance lists and locates all uses of specific words by an author in either his or her entire output or just in one or more works. There are also many books that can be consulted to help identify a quotation, such as *Bartlett's Familiar Quotations*. Most of these have subject and keyword indexes besides author indexes.

Figure 10.3. Fiction Catalog

Laumer, Keith, 1925——*Continued*
Retief to the rescue. Timescape Bks. 1983
237p o.p.

LC 82-10830

Intergalactic diplomat Retief, "a two-fisted pragmatist who, unlike his bosses, doesn't mind getting his hands dirty goes out into the field to find out what's really going on. In this case, the wormlike denizens of Furtheron, known as Creepies and Crawlies, are being kept in a perpetual state of fratricidal war so their planet's mineral riches can be stolen. He then proceeds to solve the problem with a little judiciously applied force and lots of cleverness, saving the jobs of the pompous incompetents he has to work under." Publ Wkly

Retief's ransom; a science fiction novel.
Putnam 1971 189p o.p.
In this novel Retief, the galaxy's least conventional diplomat, is a cunning arbiter in an intergalactic real estate squabble. The inhabitants of Lumbaga were virtually immortal, hopelessly eccentric conglomerations of free-living organs, whose sole hobby was mayhem, individual or in groups. This unpromising corner of the universe attracts the colonialistic eye of the rival planets, Terra and Groac. The fiendish Groaci disturb the balance of power by creating a race of super-Lumbagans

Laurence, Margaret, 1926-1987
A jest of God. Knopf 1966 240p o.p.
Rachel Cameron, a provincial spinster schoolteacher in Manitoba is trapped between a shallow mother and young children from whom she can expect no more than enforced attention. At a crucial stage of emotional life, a love affair causes her baffling pain and abandoned joyousness. Her knowledge of herself as a woman capable of using thwarted sexual energies unexpectedly provides the strength to take her first steps toward self-liberation
"Mrs. Laurence is not writing of a typical woman, but of an individual whose life patterns are commmon to many, and she does so with great insight and poetic emotion." Libr J

To locate reviews of movies, plays, television shows or other performances, follow the same general procedure used for finding book reviews. Reviews are most likely to be found in newspapers and periodicals and the subject headings should name the type of performance: Moving Pictures—Reviews. Libraries have not gotten around to using the simpler terms Films or Movies. To find plot summaries, use the catalog or check to see if the library owns some Magill sets, such as

Masterplot. These sets include the characters in the story plus a short summary of the plot. They are not adequate substitutes for reading the work but may help to refresh the memory.

Remember, before using an unfamiliar index, guide, bibliography or other reference tool, read the introductory information to figure out the organization of the work, included or excluded materials, and scope or other limitations of the work being consulted.

Exercises for Chapter 10

1. Using the catalog, identify and record the indexes of various literary forms owned by your library.
2. Using the general information in this chapter and using what you have learned in earlier chapters, answer the following questions. List the sources used to answer the questions.
   (A) Where can you find a copy of the poem "Two dogs have I" by Ogden Nash?
   (B) Find the titles and locations of three short stories written by Mark Twain.
   (C) Find two book reviews of *Hunt for Red October* by Tom Clancy.
   (D) Locate two reviews of the movie *Hunt for Red October.*
   (E) Find three plays written by Neil Simon including productions for stage, radio and television. Locate the reviews for one of them.
   (F) Find an analysis or criticism of two works by Mark Twain.
   (G) Find a plot summary of a novel by James Fenimore Cooper.

Important Terms in Chapter 10

concordance   anthology
explicator

Important Books for Chapter 10

Adams, W. Davenport. *Dictionary of English Literature: Being a Comprehensive Guide to English Authors and Their Works,* 2d cd. London: Casall, Petter and Galpin, 1966.

American Poetry Index: An Author and Title Index to Poetry by Americans in Single Author Collections. V. 1– , 1981–82, ed. by Editorial Board, Granger Book Co. Great Neck, NY: Granger, 1983.

Bartlett, John. *Familiar Quotations: A Collection of Passages, Phrases, and Proverbs Traced to Their Sources in Ancient and Modern Literature.* Ed. by Emily Morrison Beck and the editorial staff of Little, Brown and Company. Boston: Little Brown, 1980. Fifteenth and 125th anniversary ed. rev. and enl.

Carruth, Gorton, and Eugene Ehrlich. *The Harper Book of American Quotations.* New York: Harper & Row, 1988.

Essay and General Literature Index, 1900–1903: An Index to About 40,000 Essays and Articles in 2144 Volumes of Collections of Essays and Miscellaneous Works. Edited by Minnie Earl Sears and Marion Shaw. New York: H. W. Wilson, 1934. (Kept up-to-date with supplements for 1934–1940, 1941–1947, 1948–1954, 1955–1959, 1960–1964, 1965–1969, 1970–1974, 1975–1979, 1980–1984, 1985–1989 annual vols. to date.)

Fiction Catalog. 11th ed. New York: H. W. Wilson, 1986. Supplements, 1985– .

Harner, James L. *Literary Research Guide: A Guide to Reference Sources for the Study of Literatures in English and Related Topics.* New York: Modern Language Association of America, 1989.

Hazen, Edith P. *The Columbia Granger's Index to Poetry.* 9th ed. New York: Columbia University Press, 1990.

Keller, Dean Howard. *Index to Plays in Periodicals.* Rev. and enl. ed. Metuchen, NJ: Scarecrow, 1979.

Klein, Leonard S. *Encyclopedia of World Literature in the 20th Century.* New York: Frederick Ungar, 1984.

Kuntz, Joseph Marshall. *Poetry Explication: A Check List of Interpretation since 1925 of British and American Poems Past and Present.* 3rd ed. Boston: G. K. Hall, 1980.

McGarry, Daniel D., and Sarah Harriman White. *World Historical Fiction Guide: An Annotated Chronological, Geographical and Topical List of Selected Historical Novels.* 2nd ed. Metuchen, NJ: Scarecrow, 1973.

Magill, Frank N. *Masterpieces of World Literature in Digest Form*. New York: Harper, 1952–69.

Masterplots. Revised edition, ed. by Frank Magill. Englewood Cliffs, NJ: Salem Press, 1985. (Available series include: European Fiction, British Fiction, American Fiction, Short Stories, World Fiction and Drama.)

*Masterplots Annual Volume, 1954– *. Edited by Frank Magill. New York: Salem, 1955– .

Modern Language Association of America. *MLA International Bibliography of Books and Articles on the Modern Language and Literatures, 1921– *. Published as a supplement to *PMLA* (journal).

Moulton, Charles Wells. *The Library of Literary Criticism of English and American Authors*. Buffalo, NY: Moulton, 1901–05. Eight vols. Reprinted by Peter Smith, 1959.

Palmer, Alan. *Quotations in History: A Dictionary of Historical Quotations c800 to Present*. New York: Harper & Row, 1976.

Platt, Suzy. *Respectfully Quoted: A Dictionary of Quotations Requested from Congressional Research Service*. Library of Congress, Washington, DC: GPO, 1989.

Play Index, 1949–1952, 1953–1960, 1961–1967, 1968–1972, 1973–1977, 1978–1982, 1983–1987. New York: H. W. Wilson, 1949– .

Poetry Index Annual. Great Neck, NY: Granger, 1982– .

Shields, Ellen F. *Contemporary English Poetry: An Annotated Bibliography of Criticism to 1980*. New York: Garland, 1984.

Short Story Index. New York: H. W. Wilson, 1953– .

Sutton, Roberta. *Speech Index: An Index to 259 Collections of World Famous Orations and Speeches for Various Occasions*. 4th ed. Metuchen, NJ: Scarecrow, 1966. Supplements 1966–1970 by Sutton and Charity Mitchell (1972); supplement, 1971–1975 by Charity Mitchell (1977); supplement, 1966–1980 by Charity Mitchell (1982).

Teachers & Writers Handbook of Poetry Forms. Edited by Ron Padgett. New York: Teachers & Writers Collaborative, 1987.

Williams, Robert Coleman, ed. *A Concordance to the Collected Poems of Dylan Thomas*. Lincoln: University of Nebraska Press, 1966.

11. Governmental Information and Government Documents

Objectives

After studying this chapter the student shall be able to
- find names and addresses of congressmen and state officials in any district in any state
- find the name, address and organizational history of any federal agency
- find information about function and membership of any congressional committee
- use sources to locate data on local governments
- use the *Congressional Record* to find information on congressional proceedings
- find documents using indexes and bibliographies
- use the *Monthly Catalog* to find specific documents
- recognize the indexes and guides for documents located in the library
- determine the type of information available in indexes and directories of depositories

Governments — Local, State, Federal

This section deals with finding information about municipal, county, state or federal governments and their officials. There are many directories and guides that provide this kind of information and some examples are described in this chapter. If the library does not have these specific titles it will have similar ones. If the student is unable to locate the texts (check the H and J section in the reference section) then she should ask the librarian for assistance.

The *Municipal Year Book*, published by the International City Management Association, provides a variety of information about cities, including profiles, population statistics, types of government, salaries of employees, services provided and the names of officials (e.g., mayor, police chief and fire chief). It also includes discussions of the state regulations that affect municipalities. The volume has both textual descriptions and comparative charts. A recent publication that will have one volume for each state is titled *(name of state) Facts — Flying the Colors*, published by the same company which publishes *Taylor's Encyclopedia*. This set looks at each state, county by county and includes information concerning the economy, community services, recreation, transportation, county governments, etc. The text includes charts, photographs, population, names of small communities and many statistics. There is an explanation at the beginning of each volume that includes information on the sources used to compile the included data. The set began publication in 1984 and some of the early volumes have already been updated with new editions. Volumes for several additional states are issued each year. Another useful source of information on municipal and county governments is the *County and City Data Book*, which is published by the U.S. Bureau of the Census as a supplement to the *Statistical Abstracts of the United States.*

There are several other sources of information about state governments and elected officials. Many states publish a handbook describing the organization of the state government. For example, New York State publishes the *Manual for the Use of the Legislature of the State of New York* (commonly referred to as the "blue book"). This annual volume provides a copy of the state's constitution, a short history of the state, names of elected officials, biographies and photographs of the highest ranking members of the executive department and state legislature, and a complete organizational description of all departments of state government. These descriptions include names of department heads, office addresses and discussions of each department's responsibilities. They also include some political information, such as the names and addresses of state and county major party officeholders.

Another source of information on elected state and federal officials is *Taylor's Encyclopedia of Governmental Officials, Federal and State*. This encyclopedia includes a large variety of information about government (in easy-to-use format), such as copies of the Constitution, the Declaration of Independence, a list of all former presidents and vice presidents (with pictures of both, when available), cabinet members and their chief aides, all congressional committees including congressional membership, a list (with pictures) of Supreme Court members and former chief justices, and names of all judges in the federal court system (e.g., district courts, courts of appeals, claims, etc.). This encyclopedia also includes names, addresses, phone numbers and descriptions of U.S. independent governmental agencies. Information on each state includes a map showing state and federal election districts, with voting patterns (by major political parties), names of elected officials, and state, federal and chief state executives. There are additional charts and descriptions too numerous to include here. This encyclopedia has a new volume every two years and is updated with monthly supplements.

The federal government publishes another item, the *United States Government Manual* (formally the *United States Government Organization Manual*), annually and it is invaluable in untangling the mysteries of locating agencies within particular departments, what their functions are, where they are located (including regional offices) and who is in charge. The manual includes organizational charts that help in determining the hierarchical structure of each agency. The inclusion of regional offices with the names, addresses and phone numbers is also useful. Finally, the manual includes a comprehensive subject index that can be used to decide which agency or agencies are involved with specific tasks.

The Government Printing Office (GPO) issues the *Congressional Directory* that has a brief biography of every member of Congress. Besides the biographies, it includes the district numbers and the counties within each district. Also included are all committee assignments, statistical information about Congress, floor plans of the Capitol building, names of members of the executive branch, diplomats and consular officers in the United States, and members of the press who are entitled to admission to Congress, as well as other esoteric but useful bits of information about Congress. The *Congressional Staff Directory* contains the names of members of Congress, but its most functional feature is the listing of all the staff members who work for members of Congress and on congressional committees. The directory also lists 9,900 cities with a population of more than 1,500 along with the names of members of congress who represent the city. The key personnel aides to the executive branch are recorded with the office addresses, titles and phone numbers.

The *Congressional Quarterly Almanac,* published annually, is particularly valuable in providing information on actions taken by Congress during a particular year. It also encompasses other information such as roll call votes, lobbyists and presidential messages to Congress. The summaries of legislation, background and reports of action taken provide beginning information for researching congressional action in any area.

The *Congressional Record* is issued daily and contains the complete text of presidential messages, debates and congressional speeches. It also contains votes on all bills, although the text of the bills are not included. The GPO publishes the *Record* only when Congress is in session. Indexes are published throughout the session and a cumulative index is published after the session ends. Members may add to the *Record* and this additional information, "extension of remarks," may be included as an appendix but may be omitted from the final edition of the *Record.*

The format, order of information and indexing have varied since the *Record* began in 1873, so one should read the introductory remarks before using the *Record* or its indexes. For materials before 1873 the following titles should be consulted: *Debates and Proceedings, Annals of Congress* (1789–1824); *Register of Debates* (1824–1837); and *Congressional Globe* (1833–1873). They are published in both microfilm and paper copy.

Government Documents

Governments at all levels publish many documents. The United States government documents are usually easier to identify and locate than those of small municipalities or county governments. Most state governments publish checklists of their publications which simply identify publications. Libraries designated as "depositories," receive documents free of charge from municipal, county, state or federal governments.

The scope and quality of holdings in a library depend on a variety of factors, such as the date of institution and how heavily the public uses the holdings. Theft, damage and misplacement cause document loss. Some depositories do not receive all documents. These libraries are designated as selective depositories, since they choose only those documents they wish to receive. Libraries have indexes and guides to documents and directories of depository libraries. Federal documents and those reports produced by federal contracts are not copyrighted and the public is free to use them.

Federal Depository Library System

Congress created the federal depository library system by enactment in 1857 and 1858. In 1869 the position of superintendent of documents was created. The Printing Act of 1895 consolidated many previous laws and departments which dealt with aspects of preparation, printing and distribution of public documents. This act also established a "systematic program for bibliographic control" with the creation of the *Monthly Catalog* and the *Document Catalog*. This act also expanded the number of depositories and created "by law" depositories which included state libraries, governmental agency libraries and West Point and Annapolis.

This system was relatively unchanged until 1962 when the Depository Act of 1962 was passed.

There are 53 regional depositories which receive all items designated for depositories. Each state has a regional depository and some states have two regional depositories. There are over 1,350 selective depositories. Each congressional district is entitled to have two depositories although with changes in district boundaries over the years some districts have more than two. Executive departments of the federal government, accredited law schools, service academies and independent government agencies can request to be depositories.

Depository libraries are subject to rules concerning free access to the collection by the general public, the retaining and discarding of documents and inspection of the collection by staff from the superintendent of documents office.

Some depository items are published only in paper format, others only in microform or magnetic format and others are available in either paper or microform format (in which case the depository library can choose which format it prefers).

Figure 11.1
U.S. Monthly Catalog of Government Publications

forations.]   * Paper, $22.20 (basic manual and supplementary material for an indefinite period) ; add $5.50 for foreign mailing. ● Item 30–A–4   A 101.6/2 : 973/ch.1–8/rep.

00053 Meat and poultry inspection regulations, Change 8. Dec. 8, 1973. [8] p. 4° (Meat and Poultry Inspection Program.) [Issued with perforations.] * Paper, $22.00 (basic and supplementary material for indefinite period) add $5.50 for foreign mailing. ● Item 30–A–4   A 101.6/2 : 973/ch.8

00054 Screwworm. Aug. 1974. 6 p. il. 4° +   A 101.21.Scr 6

ARMS CONTROL AND DISARMAMENT AGENCY
Washington, DC   20451

00055 Arms limitation agreements, July 1974 summit. [July 1974.] 8 p. il. 4° ([Publication 73.])   +   AC 1.2 : Ar 5/5

00056 Documents on disarmament, 1972 [with bibliography ; compiled by Robert W. Lambert and others]. [May 1974.] xviii+959 p. il. ([Publication 69.])   * Paper, $7.50 (S/N 0700–00046). ● Item 865–B
AC 1.11/2 : 972

00057 SALT lexicon. [1973.] cover title, [5]+18 p. 4° #   AC 1.2 : Sa 3

00058 Statement by Fred C. Ikle, director, Arms Control and Disarmament Agency, before Subcommittee on National Security Policy and Scientific Developments of the Committee of Foreign Affairs, House of Representatives, Oct. 3, 1974. Oct. 3, 1974 6+[1] p. 4° +   AC 1.12 : Ik 6/2

ARMY DEPARTMENT, Defense Dept.
Washington, DC   20310

AMC pamphlets. (Army Materiel Command.)
00059   706–360. Engineering design handbook : Military vehicle electrical systems [with bibliographies]. June 1974. cover title, [604] p. il. 4° ● Item 322–A   D 101.22/3 : 706–360

Army Electronics Command, Fort Monmouth, N.J. : Research and development technical report ECOM (series). (Reports control symbol OSD–1366.)
00060   5512. Design concept of forward area Rawinsonde set (FARS) ; by Raymond I. Rohbiani. Oct. 1973. cover title, [2]+12+[3] p. il. 4° (Atmospheric Science Laboratory.) [Includes list of atmospheric sciences research papers.] #   D 111.9/4 : 5512
00061   5541. High resolution temperature sonde for lower atmosphere [with list of literature cited] ; by Ricardo Pena and H. N. Schwartz. May 1974. cover title, [2]+17+[8] p. il. 4° [DA task IT061102B53A–17.] #
D 111.9/4 : 5541

00062 CIF (command information film catalog) 1973 ; prepared by Army Command Information Unit. [1972.] cover title, 102 p. 4° (Office of the Chief of Information.) #   D 101.2 : F 47/973

Field manual FM (series).
00063   3–22. Fallout prediction [with list of references]. Oct. 1973. cover title, 80 p. il. 4° [Issued with perforations. Supersedes TM 3–210, Dec. 3, 1967, including all changes.] # ● Item 324   D 101.20 : 3–22

Pamphlet.
00064   18–11.   Management information systems catalog of interim data elements and codes. Mar. 1974. cover title, [345] p. 4°   [Issued with perforations.] +   ● Item 327 (Rev. 1969)   D 101.22 : 18–11
00065   360–539. See Information for Armed Forces, Office of, DoD pamphlet PA–11A.
00066   550–24. Area handbook for Lebanon [with bibliographies ; by] Harvey H. Smith [and others]. 2d edition. 1974. xlvi+354 p. il. [Prepared by Foreign Area Studies, American University. Supersedes edition of July 1969.] * Cloth, $5.70. ● Item 327 (Rev. 1969)   D 101.22 : 550–24/2
L.C. card 74–13241

@For Sale by National Technical Information Service,
   Springfield, VA 22151
●Sent to Depository Libraries

Figure 11.2.
U.S. Monthly Catalog of Government Publications

HEALTH AND HUMAN SERVICES
DEPARTMENT
Washington, DC 20201

91-11384

HE 1.2:Se 6/2

Services benefits for older persons : are you eligible? — [Washington, D.C.?] : Dept. of Health and Human Services, [1990]
[10] p. ; 21 cm. — (Department of Health and Human Services pub. ; no. 10951) Cover title. Shipping list no.: 90-735-P. "September 1990"—P. [4] of cover. ●Item 445
1. Aged — Medical care — United States. 2. Old age assistance — United States. 3. Social security beneficiaries — United States. I. United States. Dept. of Health and Human Services. II. Series: DHHS publication ; no. 10951. OCLC 23095394

SOCIAL SECURITY ADMINISTRATION
Health and Human Services Dept.
Baltimore, MD 21235

91-11385

HE 3.94:990

Fast facts & figures about social security. [Washington, D.C.] : U.S. Dept. of Health and Human Services, Social Security Administration, Office of Policy, Office of Research & Statistics : Supt. of Docs., U.S. G.P.O., [1986?- Supt. of Docs., U.S. Govt. Print. Off., Washington, DC 20402-9325
v. : col. ill. ; 22 cm. (SSA publication ; no. 13-11785)
Annual
$2.25
[1986]- Shipping list no.: 91-061-P. 1990. ●Item 516 S/N 017-070-00450-4 @ GPO
·1. Social security — United States — Statistics — Periodicals. I. United States. Social Security Administration. Office of Research and Statistics. II. Series. HD7123.F37 89-644320 368.4/3/00973021 /20 OCLC 20667525

SuDoc Classification System

Government documents are not harder to use or find, they are just organized differently. Unlike the Dewey Decimal or Library of Congress classification systems which arrange materials by subject, the SuDoc system is a provenance (or hierarchy) system. This system arranges material by the issuing agency and its various departments. The documents are arranged in a hierarchy order for each agency. They are specified as follows: parent agency, subagency, series or generic type, individual publication and date. See figures 11.1 and 11.2 from the

Monthly Catalog and note that the departments names are in the center of the column. The SuDoc number is also in heavy black type. It begins with one or two letters to identify the agency (see Figure 11.2). The HE is for the Health and Human Services Agency. The number after the letter(s) and before the decimal indicate the level, e.g. 1 for cabinet level document. The number after the decimal indicates the type of document, e.g. directive, report, newsletter, etc. As with the Dewey and LC systems there are charts noting the numbers used for departmental levels and types of documents. The numbers and letters after the colon provide information about the date of publication and the format of the document, e.g. 990 means published in 1990. Formats can be paper, microform, magnetic tape, etc. Each format has a specific number. The frequent reorganization within the federal government sometimes causes disorder with this system.

Government Printing Office (GPO)

The Printing Act of 1860 created the GPO and it opened on March 4, 1861. The GPO is officially an agency of the legislative branch but the president appoints the public printer with the consent of Congress. The public printer and the GPO are accountable to that body. The office of superintendent of documents was established on March 3, 1869, as a part of the Department of the Interior and transferred to the GPO in 1895. The Congressional Joint Committee on Printing (JCP) is a sort of board of directors for the GPO.

The GPO is the largest publisher in the United States and perhaps in the world. It acts like other publishers and also prints many items. Due to the large volume of material to be printed, the GPO contracts out many of the printing jobs to small printing companies. It coordinates the operations from the Washington, D.C. offices. There are also 13 regional printing offices as well as the Consumer Information Office in Pueblo, Colorado which acts as a distributor. The GPO also operates some bookstores which sell government documents. Some bookstore chains also stock some government documents.

The 1895 law allows the superintendent of documents to sell documents and the GPO selects titles to include in the sales program. Currently there is a formula for determining the sale price: cost + 50 percent. This sales program generates revenue for the GPO and allows the agency to support the documents sent free to depository libraries and those documents distributed to the general public free of charge (many through the center in Pueblo). Recently the GPO made some changes in its system of payment and now accepts major credit cards besides prepayment and deposit accounts. The GPO sells many documents to commercial publishers which then may be reprinted and sold or used in other ways. For example, the census material, in magnetic format, is sold to many types of corporations that can manipulate the data for their own use. All these sales operations generate revenue that makes the GPO a self-sustaining operation, requiring little or no taxpayer funds. Due to cutbacks in the Reagan administration, fewer documents (titles) were published and print runs were smaller thus curtailing the public's access to some information.

National Technical Information Service (NTIS)

The NTIS in the Commerce Department was established on September 2, 1970. Its general purpose is to simplify and improve access to data files of scientific literature, technical reports, etc., from federal agencies and federal contractors. Much of the material available from NTIS may not be available from depository libraries. Not all unclassified documents are designated as depository items. The NTIS is a distributor of some government documents and reports, etc., of research done on government contracts (not considered to be government documents). These materials are in various formats: paper copy, microform, magnetic and CD. The NTIS is required by law to recover its costs from the sale of its documents so it is more expensive to purchase from NTIS than from the GPO. Sometimes, especially with reports of research done on government contracts, documents are available sooner from NTIS than from the GPO. Some of the reports available from NTIS are prepared and published by individuals, corporations, universities, etc., that have done research using federal funds.

The *Government Reports Announcements and Index* (GRA&I) is the main bibliographic tool used to locate and identify material at NTIS. NTIS publishes GRA&I twice monthly with annual accumulations. Its indexes include keyword, personal author, corporate author and contract/grant number. Information for ordering, including codes, prices, format, etc., is also included.

Federal Documents

Most documents sought by library users are United States government publications. The federal documents, most of which are published by the GPO, are indexed and identified in several publications. One can identify early dated documents by using a *Descriptive Catalogue of Government Publications of the United States, September 5, 1774–March 4, 1881,* compiled by Perley Poore, 1885. The *Comprehensive Index to Publications of the United States, 1881–1894* by John G. Ames, 1905, identifies documents in the years following. The current index, *Monthly Catalog of Government Publications* (*Monthly Cat* for short) first appeared in 1895 and is still published monthly. Collections also contain specific checklists and catalogs of federal documents that deal with subjects such as forestry or are records of agencies or departments, such as congressional hearings.

Before using the *Monthly Cat,* one should examine the instructions at the beginning of the volume because the format and indexing have changed from time to time. Each monthly issue is arranged alphabetically by agency issuing the document. Each document is given a number similar to an abstract number, called the *Monthly Cat* number. This number appears in the left margin for each document or column of each page. Early volumes of the *Monthly Cat* had only an annual subject index, but since 1975 additional indexes such as title and report indexes have been added. This makes it easier to identify documents (see figures 11.1 and 11.2). Note the *Monthly Cat* number in the left margin. After the end of the entry in the right hand margin is another indicator, usually a combination of letters and numbers. This is the "SuDoc" number, assigned by the superintendent of documents who is in charge of the GPO and other government printing operations. Depository libraries usually do not catalog their documents but file them by the SuDoc number, which in a sense is the "call" number. The other symbols in the entry show additional information such as where to purchase a copy of the document and its depository status.

Figure 11.2 illustrates the latest format used in the *Monthly Cat.* The *Monthly Cat* number still appears at the left of each entry but the SuDoc number appears in bold at the beginning of each entry. The entries are in the format of a catalog card and each entry still contains information about its depository status. The large black dot shows depository items. The last line of each entry is an OCLC number. The

OCLC system will be discussed in Chapter 14. Since 1976 when the *Monthly Cat* changed its format it has been available on magnetic tape. Some large libraries that also have large depository collections like the New York State Library have loaded the tape for the monthly catalog into their On-Line Public Catalog (OPAC). This ensures that users have access to all the information in the *Monthly Cat* since 1976 by using the OPAC only. Easier access to government documents is thus made possible as well as making more individuals aware of the variety of information available from documents. Since documents are not usually in the catalog, many students and faculty forget that they are a valuable source of information. The *Monthly Cat* is also available in some libraries on CDs, adding ways of searching for documents.

The *Index to U.S. Government Periodicals* is published commercially and is an index to 185 selected periodicals published by the U.S. government. The index is published quarterly with annual accumulations. Its format is similar to that used by the Wilson indexes discussed in Chapter 8.

The Congressional Information Services (CIS) publishes a variety of reference books about government and indexes to documents, including the *American Statistics Index, CIS/Index* and *CIS Serials Set Index*. CIS publications all include lengthy explanations and examples of entries and this introductory material should be read before the student uses any CIS publication for the first time. As its title suggests, *American Statistics Index* presents statistics published by the federal government. Many departments and agencies besides the Census Bureau publish statistics. The *CIS/Index* has several sections: Legislative Histories of U.S. Public Laws, Index to Congressional Publications and Public Laws, and Abstracts of Congressional Publications. This index is published monthly with an annual accumulation, the *CIS/Annual*. Multi-year indexes are available for the index volumes, but not the abstract volumes. The *U.S. Serial Set* has been known by various names and has changed in format and content. Generally the set consists of congressional publications; reports and documents of both house and senate, treaty documents and senate executive reports. This set is a primary source for locating the texts of reports, treaties, bill, special reports, etc. The numbering system in the *U.S. Serial Set* has changed from time to time so it is important to consult the introductory material. Since 1970 CIS has provided full-text microfiche for all publications covered in CIS indexes. Many libraries (not necessarily depositories) have purchased these microfiche. CIS uses its own numbering system for its microfiche edition of the *U.S. Serial Set* and those numbers will also appear in the CIS indexes.

There are other indexes to documents that are subject specific and often prepared by specific agencies, for example, *Scientific and Technical Aerospace Reports* (STAR) produced at NASA.

Educational Resources Information Center (ERIC)

The collecting, abstracting, indexing, distribution, etc., of significant education related reports and journal articles is the mission of ERIC, the national system of clearinghouses located at universities and or professional organizations. *Resources in Education* (RIE) (see Figure 11.3), a GPO publication, is an abstracting journal providing bibliographic information and identification of the reports, published and unpublished. Libraries may subscribe to ERIC and receive copies of the reports in microfiche format. The fiche are usually filed by the number found at the beginning of each entry in RIE (see Figure 11.3) the ERIC document number. The numbering system is similar to but not identical to the system used in the *Monthly Cat.* Each entry includes general bibliographic information and an abstract the same as other abstracting sources discussed in Chapter 8. The entries also contain other information such as contract numbers, where to get paper copies and their cost, descriptors (useful for searching ERIC on-line for related items), etc.

Current Index to Journals in Education published by Oryx Press is the second index providing access to materials collected by ERIC. This publication indexes approximately 750 journals/serials, and issues monthly and semi-annual accumulations. The information included in each entry is typical of other abstracting services discussed in Chapter 8 with the addition of a list of descriptors.

Students also may identify ERIC documents by searching the indexes via on-line vendors, such as DIALOG, or on CDs available in many libraries. To help in searching the ERIC files on-line or via CDs it is useful to consult the *Thesaurus of ERIC Descriptors* (Figure 11.4).

Figure 11.3. Resources in Education

ED 323 901   HE 023 913
Broome, Benjamin J.   And Others
Long-Range Planning in a University Setting: A
Case Study.
Pub Date—Nov 89
Note—38p.; Paper presented at the Annual Meet-
ing of the Speech Communication Association
(75th, San Francisco, CA, November 18-21,
1989).
Pub Type— Speeches / Meeting Papers (150) — Re-
ports - Evaluative (142)
EDRS Price - MF01/PC02 Plus Postage.
Descriptors—Case Studies. *College Planning, De-
partments, Higher Education, *Long Range Plan-
ning,   *Mission   Statements,   Models,
*Organizational Objectives, Policy Formation,
Speech Communication
Identifiers—*George Mason University VA, Organizational Research, *Strategic Planning
A case study is presented that used the methods
of Generic Design Science to conduct strategic
planning for the Department of Communication at
George Mason University, Fairfax, Virginia. Applied in the context of an academic environment,
the methods yielded a comprehensive management
and planning design for focusing administration and
faculty efforts over a 3-year period. The products of
the design work include: (1) an intent structure of
objectives; (2) alternative options for accomplishing
the objectives; (3) a 3-year departmental plan; and
(4) a mission statement. In the judgment of the departmental chair, the approach has been of benefit
to the department in establishing a standard for con-
tinuous planning and design. Equally important, the
faculty has identified priorities to guide the development of curriculum, research, and allocation of resources. A mission statement, the structural model,
and an options profile are included. Contains nine
references. (Author / GLR)

Figure 11.4. Thesaurus of ERIC Descriptors

LEGENDS   *Jul. 1966*
      CIJE: 138   RIE: 317   GC: 430
BT   Literary Genres
      Literature
RT   American Indian Literature
      Classical Literature
      Didacticism
      Epics
      Fairy Tales
      Fiction
      Folk Culture
      Medieval Literature
      Metaphors
      Mythology

LEGISLATION   *Jul. 1966*
      CIJE: 778   RIE: 1231   GC: 610
SN   The enactments of, or matters under
      consideration by, a legislative body
      (note use a more specific term if pos-
      sible)
NT   Civil Rights Legislation
      Discriminatory Legislation
      Educational Legislation
      Federal Legislation
      Labor Legislation
      Local Legislation
      Minimum Wage Legislation
      Public Health Legislation
      Recreation Legislation
      State Legislation
RT   Compliance (Legal)
      Government (Administrative Body)
      Hearings
      Laws
      Legislators
      Lobbying
      Policy Formation
      Political Issues
      Politics
      Public Policy

Legislative Discrimination
use DISCRIMINATORY LEGISLATION

Legislative Reference Libraries (1968 1980)
use LAW LIBRARIES

Exercises for Chapter 11

1. Using the catalog, list the indexes and guides to documents in your library. Record call numbers for future reference.
2. Using the *Monthly Catalog,* answer the following questions.
   (A) Check the subject index for 1975, 1980, 1985 and 1990 for documents issued each year on solar energy.
      1. Compare the number of documents issued each year.
      2. What agency issued the most documents?
      3. Are most of the documents found in depository libraries?
   (B) Locate and identify the documents dealing with the Iran Contra affair.
3. Choose one U.S. senator from your home state and locate the following information:
   (A) Washington address
   (B) committee assignments
   (C) names of chief aids
4. Find the following information:
   (A) The name of the vice president under Harry Truman.
   (B) The location of the Federal Reserve Banks.
   (C) The name of the chief judge in your state.
5. Find the population of your home county. List all the sources in your library which provide this information. You should include all sources discussed in previous chapters.

Important Terms in Chapter 11

Monthly Catalog *number*   *depository library*
SuDoc *number*   *GPO*
Superintendent of Documents   *municipality*
NTIS   *ERIC*
CIS

Important Books for Chapter 11

Guides

Clark, Carol Lea. *A Citizen's Directory: Who to Contact to Get Things Done.* New York: Facts on File, 1983.

Directory of Government Document Collections and Librarians, 4th ed. Government Documents Roundtable, American Library Association, ed. by Barbara Kile and Audrey Taylor. Washington, DC: Congressional Information Service, 1984.

Garner, Diane L. *The Complete Guide to Citing Government Documents: A Manual for Writers and Librarians.* Government Documents Roundtable, American Library Association. Washington, DC: Congressional Information Services, 1984.

Government Reference Books. Edited by LeRoy Schwarzkopf. Littleton, CO: Libraries Unlimited, 1970– . (Biennial guide to U.S. government publications.)

Houston, James E. ed. *Thesaurus of ERIC Descriptors.* 12th ed., Phoenix, AZ: Oryx, 1990.

Leidy, William Philip. *A Popular Guide to Government Publications,* 4th ed. New York: Columbia University Press, 1976.

Mayros, Van, and Michael D. Werner. *Guide to Information from Government Sources.* Radnor, PA: Chilton Books, 1983.

Morehead, Joe. *Introduction to United States Public Documents.* 3rd ed. Littleton, CO: Libraries Unlimited, 1981.

Municipal Government Reference Sources: Publications and Collections. Edited for the American Association Government Roundtable by Peter Hernon. New York: R. R. Bowker, 1978.

Parish, David. *State Government Reference Publications,* 2nd ed. Littleton, CO: Libraries Unlimited, 1981.

Pokorny, Elizabeth J. *U.S. Government Documents: A Practical Guide for Non-Professionals in Academic and Public Libraries.* Englewood, CO: Libraries Unlimited, 1989.

Ross, John M. *How to Use Major Indexes to U.S. Government Publications.* Chicago, IL: American Library Association, 1989.

Wilcox, Jerome Kear. *Manual on the Use of State Publications.* Chicago: American Library Association, 1940.

U.S. Publications—Indexes

American Statistics Index. V. 1– , 1973– . Washington, DC: Congressional Information Service, 1973– .

Ames, John G. *Comprehensive Index to the Publications of the United States Government, 1881–1893*. Washington, DC: GOP, 1976.

CIS/Index. V. 1– , 1970– . Bethesda, MD: Congressional Information Service, 1970– .

Congressional Record: Containing the Proceedings and Debates of the 43 Congress—March 4, 1987– . Washington, DC: GOP, 1973– . V. 1– . (Issues daily while Congress is in session. Revised, bound form issued at the end of each session.)

Current Index to Journals in Education. Phoenix, AZ: Oryx, 1969– .

Government Reports Announcements & Index. V. 75– , 1975– . Springfield, VA: U.S. Department of Commerce, NTIS, 1975– . Earlier volumes have various titles.

Index to Annals of the Congress of the United States, 1st Congress Through 18th Congress, 1789–1824. Washington, DC: U.S. Historical Documents Institution, 1970 (reprint ed.).

Index to the Register of Debates in Congress. Containing Indexes to the Appendices, 18th Congress, 1st Session, 1824–1837. Washington, DC: Gales & Seaton, 1976. Compiled from authentic materials (reprint ed.).

Index to U.S. Government Periodicals, 1970– . Chicago: Infodata International, 1970– .

Indexes to the Congressional Globe, 23rd Congress to the 42nd Congress, Dec. 2, 1833–March 3, 1873. Washington, DC: Office of the Congressional Globe, 1970. (Reprint of 1834–73 ed.)

Poore, Benjamin Perley. A *Descriptive Catalogue of the Government Publications of the United States, Sept. 5, 1774–March 4, 1881*. Comp. by order of Congress. Washington, DC: GOP, 1885.

Resources in Education. Phoenix, AZ: Oryx, 1980– .

Scientific & Technical Aerospace Reports. National Aeronautics & Space Administration. *STAR, and Abstract Journal*. V. 1– , 1963– . Washington, DC: GOP, 1963– .

United Nations Publication

Brimmer, Brenda, et al. A *Guide to the Use of the United Nations Documents*. Dobbs Ferry, NY: Oceana, 1962.

A *Comprehensive Handbook of the United Nations: A Documentary Presentation in Two Volumes.* Compiled and edited by Minchuan Ku. New York: Monarch Press, 1978.

McConaughy, John Bothwell, and Hazel Janet Blanks. *A Student's Guide to United Nations Documents and Their Use.* New York: Council on International Relations and United Nations Affairs, 1969.

United Nations and Dag Hammarskjold Library. *Checklist of United Nations Documents, 1946–1949.* New York, 1949–1953.

————— and —————. *United Nations Documents Index.* New York, pub. monthly beginning with 1950.

————— and —————. Secretary-General. *Public Papers of the Secretaries-General of the United Nations.* Andrew W. Cordier, Wilder Foote, and Max Harrelson, eds. New York: Columbia University Press, 1969–1977 (8 vols.).

Winton, Harry N. M., comp. *Publications of the United Nations System: A Reference Guide.* New York: R. R. Bowker, 1972.

Guides to Government and Elected Officials

Congressional Quarterly Almanac, a Service for Editors and Commentators. V. 1– , 1945– . Washington, DC: Congressional Quarterly, 1945– .

Congressional Staff Directory, 1959– . Indianapolis: Bobbs-Merrill, 1959– .

Municipal Year Book: An Authoritative Resume of Activities and Statistical Data of American Cities. Washington, DC: International City Management Association, 1934– .

New York Department of State. *Manual for the Use of the Legislature of the State of New York, 1840– .* Albany, 1840– .

Official Congressional Directory. Washington, DC: GOP, 1900– .

State Blue Books, Legislative Manuals and Reference Publications: A Selective Bibliography. Edited by Lynn Hellebust. Topeka, KS: Government Research Service, 1990.

Taylor's Encyclopedia of Government Officials, Federal and State.
V. 1- , 1967– . Dallas: Political research, 1967/68– .

United States Bureau of the Census. *County and City Data Book.*
1949– . Washington, DC: GOP, 1949– .

United States Manual 1973– . Federal Register, Washington, DC:
GOP, 1973– . (Earlier title, *United States Government Organization Manual.*)

12. Biography

Objectives

After studying this chapter the student shall be able to
- list the biographical sources the library holds
- figure out what each source contains
- locate biographical information for specific individuals

General Information

Students often think of biographies as book-length histories of individuals, but there are many sources that provide brief biographical information. Often the only bit of information needed is a current address, date of birth, place of employment or current occupation. To find the sources of biography in the library, one checks the catalog under the subject Biography. There is an extensive list of entries under the broad heading Biography and entries with subheadings such as Biography—Dictionaries. The student should take a brief cursory look through all the entries. To find a book-length biography of a specific person, look in the catalog under the individual's name as a subject, e.g., Lincoln, Abraham. Those which are subject entries refer to books with biographical information. When looking through the entries under the subject heading Biography one will find some biographical indexes, some for biographical dictionaries and some for biographical encyclopedias. Each of these sources includes many individuals. A few examples of biographical sources available in many libraries are listed below.

Figure 12.1. Biography Index

Brown, Christy, 1932-1981, Irish author
  Brown, Christy. My left foot. Minerva 1990 184p
Brown, Clarence, 1890-1987, motion picture director and
    producer
  Rimoldi, O. A. Clarence Brown. il *Films Rev* 41:418-23
    Ag/S '90; 41:450-7 O '90
Brown, Dee Alexander, author
  Hagen, Lyman B. Dee Brown. Boise State Univ. 1990
    52p bibl
  Major 20th-century writers; a selection of sketches from
    Contemporary authors; Bryan Ryan, editor. Gale Res.
    1991 p411-13 bibl
Brown, Eleanor McMillen, 1890-1991, interior designer
  Obituary
    N Y Times por pA-19 F 1 '91
Brown, George Mackay, Scottish author and poet
  Major 20th-century writers; a selection of sketches from
    Contemporary authors; Bryan Ryan, editor. Gale Res.
    1991 p414-15 bibl -
Brown, Ivory Lee, football player
  Murphy, A. Ivory Lee Brown. por *Sports Illus* 73:104
    S 3 '90
Brown, James, singer
  Hirshey, G. James Brown. il pors *Roll Stone* p98-9+
    Ag 23 '90
Brown, Joan, 1938-1990, painter
  Obituary
    N Y Times Biogr Serv 21:1012 O '90
Brown, Julie, singer and comedienne
  Julie Brown, by herself. por *Gentlemens Q* 60:140-1
    Jl '90
Brown, Kathleen, lawyer
  Schine, E. The Brown to watch in California. por *Bus
    Week* p158 N 5 '90
Brown, Lee Patrick, police commissioner
  People to watch. il por *U S News World Rep* 109:72-5+
    D 31 '90-Ja 7 '91

Indexes

Biography Index, (Figure 12.1) published by the H. W. Wilson Company, is a quarterly index to biographical information in books and periodicals. Multi-year volumes replace quarterly and annual volumes. They are arranged alphabetically by the name of the biographee, and at the back of the volume is a list of the biographees arranged by profession and occupation. The format is the same as other Wilson indexes discussed in earlier chapters.

The *Biography and Genealogy Master Index* is an index to biographies in more than 250 biographical dictionaries and Who's Whos. The base set was published in 1981 and there are in five-year cumulations, for 1981 to 1985 and 1986 to 1990. This set was preceded by the *Biographical Dictionaries Master Index* published in 1975 and 1976. This set of indexes saves time and eliminates guessing which biographical dictionaries should be consulted.

Marquis Publications

Most of the biographical dictionaries with a title beginning with "Who's Who in . . ." are published by Marquis. They publish an index to all their biographical publications, *Marquis Who's Who Publications, Index to Who's Who Book*. The 1990 edition includes over 253,500 individuals listed in the latest edition of 13 different Who's Who titles. Not all books in the Who's Who series are published annually. Perhaps the most familiar in the Who's Who series is *Who's Who in America* (Figure 12.2). The volumes in this series include brief biographical information about notable living Americans. Other Marquis Who's Who volumes are limited in one way or another: regional areas (*Who's Who in the East*) for instance; professions (*Who's Who in Finance and Industry*); or special categories (*Who's Who in American Women*). Marquis also publishes historical volumes as companions to *Who's Who in America*. These volumes, entitled *Who Was Who in America*, began coverage (of notable Americans) with the year 1607.

Authors

There are several sources of biographical information that deal specifically with authors. The Gale Research Company publishes the *Author Biographies Master Index*, which is similar to the *Biography and Genealogy Master Index* discussed above. Another useful Gale publication is *Contemporary Authors* (Figure 12.3), which includes authors of nontechnical works, living or deceased. As of volume 138, 1993, the set includes more than 96,000 authors. A cumulative index for volumes 1 to 138 is available as a separate volume. Other author biographical dictionaries are *European Authors, 1000–1900*, edited by Stanley J. Kunitz and Vineta Colby, *Twentieth Century Authors* (with supplements), edited by Stanley J. Kuntz and Howard Haycraft, and *World Authors, 1950–70* (supplement to previous title), edited by John Wakeman.

Figure 12.2. Who's Who in America

MOYER, ALAN DEAN, newspaper editor: b. Galva, Iowa. Sept. 4, 1928; s. Clifford Lee and Harriet (Jacques) M.; m. Patricia Helen Krecker, July 15, 1950: children: Virginia, Stanley, Glenn. BS in Journalism. U. Iowa, 1950. Reporter, copy editor Wis. State Jour., Madison, 1950-53; reporter, photographer Bartlesville (Okla.) Examiner-Enterprise, 1953; telegraph editor Abilene (Tex.) Reporter-News, 1954-55; makeup editor Cleve. Plain Dealer, 1955-63; mng. editor Wichita (Kans.) Eagle, 1963-70; exec. editor Wichita Eagle and Beacon, 1970-73; mng. editor Phoenix Gazette, 1973-82, Ariz. Republic, 1982-89: ret. 1989; pres., dir. Wichita Profl. Baseball, Inc., 1969-75; mem. jury Pulitzer Prizes, 1973-74, 85, 86, 88. Mem AP Mng. Editors Assn. (dir. 1973-78). Am. Soc. Newspaper Editors, Wichita Area C. of C. (dir. 1970-72), Sigma Delta Chi. Office: Phoenix Newspaper Inc 120 E Van Buren St Phoenix AZ 85004

MOYER, F. STANTON, private investor; b. Phila., June 7, 1929; s. Edward T. and Beatrice (Stanton) M.; m. Ann P. Stovell, May 16, 1953: children: Edward E., Alice E. B.S. in Econs., U. Pa., 1951. Registered rep. Smith, Barney & Co., Phila., 1951-54, Kidder, Peabody & Co., Phila., 1954-60; mgr. corp. dept. Blyth Eastman Dillon & Co., Inc. (formerly Eastman Dillon, Union Securities & Co.), Phila., 1960-65; instl. sales mgr. Blyth Eastman Dillon & Co., Inc. (formerly Eastman Dillon, Union Securities & Co.), 1965-67, gen. partner, 1967-71, 1st v.p., 1971-74, sr. v.p., 1974-80; v.p., resident officer Kidder, Peabody & Co. Inc., Phila., 1980-86; chmn. Pa. Mcht. Group Ltd., Radnor, 1987-88; exec. v.p. Rorer Asset Mgmt. Co., Phila., 1988—, E.C. Rorer & Co., Inc., 1990—. Trustee U. Pa., 1978-83, Hosp. of U. Pa., 1978-87; bd. dirs. Atwater Kent Mus., Phila., 1983-88. Mem. Delta Psi. Republican. Episcopalian. Clubs: Racquet (Phila.), St. Anthony (Phila.); Merion Cricket (Haverford, Pa.), Gulph Mills Golf (King of Prussia, Pa.). Home: 37 Evans Ln Haverford PA 19041 Office: Rorer Asset Mgmt Co 5150 One Liberty Pl PHiladelphia PA 19103

MOYER, GORDON VAN ZANDT, retired pharmaceutical executive, educator; b. Glenside, Pa., Mar. 27, 1921; s. Winfield Tyson and Lena (Van Zandt) M.; m. Shirley Edna Cummings. Mar. 26, 1949; children: Carol Moyer Haldy, Nancy, Lucille Moyer Dubas. Janet, Geoffrey. B.S., U. Pa., 1942, M.B.A., 1949. Asst. to treas. Rohm & Haas Co., Phila., 1947-52; treas. Frank H. Fleer Corp., Phila., 1952-62, William H. Rorer Inc., Fort Washington, Pa., 1962-69; v.p. fin. William H. Rorer Inc., 1969-71; sr. v.p., treas. Rorer Group Inc. (formerly Rorer-Amchem, Inc.), Fort Washington, Pa., 1972-80; pres. Rorer Group Inc. (formerly Rorer-Amchem, Inc.), 1980-84, also dir.; adj. prof. acctg. Wharton Sch., U. Pa. 1984—; bd. dirs. Harleysville Group Inc. Bd. dirs. Fox Chase Cancer Ctr. Served with USNR, 1943-46. Mem. Fin. Execs. Inst. (pres. Phila. 1970-71). Presbyterian (deacon 1966-72. elder 1977-83, trustee 1986—). Club: Merion Golf. Home: 820 Deerfield Ln Bryn Mawr PA 19010 Office: 500 Virginia Dr Fort Washington PA 19034*

Additional Information

There are more specific biographical dictionaries published. Some include only living persons, some only deceased, some are combined lists, some are by profession and some by country or geographical region. Some examples include: *American Men and Women of Science, Dictionary of American Biography, Current Biography,* and *Who's Who in the Socialist Countries of Europe.* For more information about biographical dictionaries in the library consult one or more of the guides to references sources discussed earlier. *Guide to Reference Books,* edited by Sheehy, includes many biographical dictionaries with descriptions (see its section AJ pp. 279-313, 10th edition).

Figure 12.3. Contemporary Authors

FITZPATRICK, Vincent (dePaul III) 1950-

PERSONAL: Born June 18, 1950, in Baltimore, Md.; son of Vincent, Jr., and Margaret S. Fitzpatrick; married Carolyn Ellsworth Henley, August 8, 1981. *Education:* University of Virginia, B.A., 1972; State University of New York at Stony Brook, M.A., 1974, Ph.D., 1979. *Avocational interests:* Officiating high school and college basketball games.

ADDRESSES: Office—Department of Humanities, Enoch Pratt Free Library, 400 Cathedral St., Baltimore, Md. 21201.

CAREER: Enoch Pratt Free Library, Baltimore, Md., assistant curator of H. L. Mencken Collection, 1980—.

WRITINGS:

(Contributor) Heinz Moos and Thomas Piltz, editors, *Three Hundred Years of German Immigrants in North America,* Heinz Moos Verlag, 1982.
H. L. M., the Mencken Bibliography: A Second Ten-Year Supplement, 1972-1981, Enoch Pratt Free Library, 1986.
(Contributor) Douglas C. Stenerson, editor, *Critical Essays on H. L. Mencken,* G. K. Hall, 1987.
H. L. Mencken, Continuum, 1989.
(Contributor) Edward Chielens, editor, *American Literary Magazines: The Twentieth Century,* Greenwood Press, 1990.
(Contributor) A. Franklin Parks and John B. Wiseman, editors, *Maryland: Unity in Diversity, Essays on Maryland Life and Culture,* Kendall/Hunt, 1990.
(With Marybeth B. Ruscica and Carolyn H. Fitzpatrick) *The Complete Sentence Workout Book,* 2nd edition, Heath, in press.

Contributor to literature and history magazines and newspapers.

WORK IN PROGRESS: A critical biography of journalist, biographer, and historian Gerald White Johnson.

Other sources of biographical information in all libraries have been discussed in previous chapters. Encyclopedias, both general and subject (see Chapter 7), have biographies. Biographical information, including obituaries, is available in newspapers. Consult the index to the newspaper. Look under "Deaths" to find obituaries. The *New York Times* has published a volume indexing all obituaries that appeared from 1858 to 1968 and a supplement for 1969 to 1978. The *Personal Name Index to the New York Times* is the best source for finding personal names (and thus biographical information) that appeared in the *New York Times.* The main set includes all names that appeared until 1974. A supplement brings the set up to 1989. The *New York*

Times does not publish or approve of the *Personal Name Index*. Another useful source of biographical information is the *Essay and General Literature Index* (see Chapter 9). Also many periodicals include biographical information. To locate biographical articles, use the periodical indexes (see Chapter 8). Biographies also may be located by using bibliographies (see Chapter 5).

Exercises for Chapter 12

1. List the biographical indexes owned by your library. Include the call numbers.
2. Using biographical indexes, biographical dictionaries and other sources owned by your library, look up the biographies of the individuals listed below. Look in at least two sources for each. Record the sources where you found the information. If the individual is not located in the first two sources, check at least three more sources. Be sure to record the name of the individual checked.
   (A) Your congressman
   (B) Your favorite author
   (C) Jacques Yves Cousteau
   (D) Dan Rather
   (E) Ben C. Wang
3. Find the name of a pianist and then locate a biography for that person.

Important Terms in Chapter 12

obituaries

Important Books for Chapter 12

American Men and Women of Science, 18th ed. New York: R. R. Bowker, 1992–1993 (8 vols.).

Author Biographies Master Index. Ed. by Dennis La Beau. Detroit: Gale Research, 1978.

Biographical Dictionaries Master Index. Ed. 1, 1975–76. Detroit: Gale Research, 1975. Supplements.

Biography and Genealogy Master Index. Gale Research, 1981– . Base volumes published in 1981. Five year cumulations for 1981 to 1985 and 1986 to 1990. Annual updates. Covers more than 250 biographical dictionaries and Who's Whos.

Biography Index: A Cumulative Index to Biographical Materials in Books and Magazines. New York: H. W. Wilson, 1947– .

Contemporary Authors: A Bio-Bibliographical Guide to Current Authors and Their Works. Detroit: Gale Research, 1962– .

Current Biography. V. 1– , 1940– . New York: H. W. Wilson, 1940– (monthly except August).

Dictionary of American Biography. Published under the auspices of the American Council of Learned Societies. New York: Scribner's; London: Milford, 1928–37. 20 vols. plus index. As of 1993 there are 8 supplementary volumes plus an index to the supplements. Supplement 8 published in 1988.

Dictionary of National Biography. Edited by Sir Leslie Stephen and Sir Sidney Lee. London: Smith Elder, 1908. 22 vols. Reprinted, 1938. Supplements.

Encyclopedia of World Biography. Palatine, IL: J. Heraty, 1987. Volumes 13–16 of the *McGraw-Hill Encyclopedia of World Biography*, 1973.

Kunitz, Stanley Jasspon, and Vineta Colby. *European Authors, 1000–1900: A Biographical Dictionary of European Literature*. New York: H. W. Wilson, 1967.

Kunitz, Stanley Jasspon, and Howard Haycroft. *Twentieth Century Authors: A Biographical Dictionary of Modern Literature*. New York: H. W. Wilson, 1942.

Marquis Who's Who Publications, Index to Who's Who Books, 1974– . Chicago, Marquis, 1975– .

New York Times Obituary Index, 1858–1968. New York: New York Times, 1970. Supplement 1969–1978, pub. 1980.

Wakeman, John. *World Authors, 1950–1970; A Companion Volume to "Twentieth Century Authors."* New York: H. W. Wilson, 1975.

Who Was Who in America: A Companion Biographical Reference Work to "Who's Who in America." Chicago: Marquis. 1963– (V. 9 is 1985–1989 published in 1989). Index 1607–1989.

Who's Who in America: A Biographical Dictionary of Notable Living Men and Women. Chicago: Marquis, 1899– (biennial).

Who's Who in Finance and Industry, 1936– . Chicago: Marquis, 1936– .

Who's Who in the East: A Biographical Dictionary of Leading Men and Women in the Eastern United States. V. 1– , 1942/43. Chicago: Marquis, 1943– .

Who's Who in the Socialists Countries of Europe: A Biographical Encyclopedia of More Than 12,600 Leading Personalities in Albania, Bulgaria, Czechoslovakia, German Democratic Republic, Hungary, Poland, Romania, Yugoslavia. New York: K. G. Saur, 1989.

Who's Who of American Women: A Biographical Dictionary of Notable Living American Women. Ed. 1– , 1958/9. Chicago: Marquis, 1958– .

13. Business and Consumer Information

Objectives

After studying this chapter the student shall be able to
- locate firms manufacturing specific products
- locate names and addresses of companies and business organizations
- locate information about specific business, industries and organizations
- use consumer-advocate publications to find information about products

General Information

This chapter deals with the location of information about manufacturers, retail stores, consumer-orientated organizations and other types of businesses. Finding and using this information is useful in job hunting, purchasing and consumer complaining. This chapter focuses on some specific reference books for business and consumer information. Besides the new sources introduced in this chapter, one also may wish to consult sources discussed in earlier chapters, for example the yellow pages of the telephone directory and the ads in newspapers.

135

Business

Thomas' Register of American Manufacturers (1990 edition with 23 volumes) has several sections. The first section (volumes 1 through 14 of the 1990 edition) is a list of products and services available from the various companies by type of company. For example, if the names of knitting mills in an area are needed, one should look in *Thomas' Register* under "knit goods," where there is a listing by states of the names and addresses of knitting mills. The next section, company profiles (volumes 15 and 16), is an alphabetical listing of companies including addresses and phone numbers. The third, and last, section (volumes 17 to 23, the "Thom Cat") contains the catalogs of about 10 percent of the included companies. If one desires a new valve for a water heater and there is no local distributor for that manufacturer, the catalog contains the address and phone number of the manufacturer. Many manufacturers' catalogs include diagrams, pictures and part numbers. The *Register* also may be useful in providing the names, addresses and phone numbers of firms involved in a specific type of business. This kind of listing is helpful to individuals looking for a job in a specific industry.

Dun & Bradstreet, an agency supplying credit information and credit ratings, publishes several useful directories. For example, their *Million Dollar Directory* lists corporations with a net worth of $1,000,000 or more. The directory lists businesses alphabetically and gives the following information for each business: the address, the phone number, the number of employees, the annual sales, the type of business and names (with titles) of the executives. There are a variety of indexes enabling the user to identify businesses by type, geographical area and executives' names. These indexes make it easy to locate firms of certain types in specific geographical areas; for example, all the photographic suppliers in New England.

Dun & Bradstreet also publishes the *Middle Market Directory*, which includes businesses whose net worth is $500,000 to $999,999. This directory lists information like the *Million Dollar Directory*.

The Moody's manuals, covering a dozen topics such as public utilities, transportation and banks and finance, give lengthy reports about the businesses included. The articles include a corporate history, information on stocks, financial status and statements, management and other information. Moody's manuals are published by Dun & Bradstreet.

The *Standard & Poor's Register of Corporations, Directors and Executives* is a directory to American and Canadian businesses and generally gives the same type of information found in the Dun & Bradstreet directories.

David Brownstone's *Where to Find Business Information* is an international listing of English language publications dealing with business and industry. It includes sources such as newsletters, trade and general periodicals, books and computerized databases. This volume is an annotated bibliography with indexes leading the user to those sources (books, newsletters and periodicals) that should provide answers to specific questions.

Organizations — Profit, Nonprofit, etc.

The *Encyclopedia of Associations* issues a new edition approximately every other year. Volume 1 (which has several physical volumes) is the *National Organizations of the United States*. It is arranged by subject (a classified list) and includes a keyword index to the organization's name. Volume 2 is *Geographic and Executive Indexes*. The geographic index section lists all organizations in volume 1 alphabetically by state and city. The executive index is a list of executives listed in volume one, arranged alphabetically by surnames. Volume 3 is *New Associations and Projects* and is a supplement to volume 1. Volume 4 is *International Organizations*. There is a seven volume guide to regional, state and local organizations. Entries in volumes 1, 3 and 4 provide the full name of the association, the address and phone number, the name of the director and a description of the association. The description may include the following types of information: date founded, number of members, number of staff, publications, committees, annual meetings and conventions, and a brief history of the organization. The keyword index enables the user to identify the organization even if only one word of the organization's name is known. The classified format provides a means of locating all organizations of a similar type without knowing the names of any specific organizations.

Consumer Information

Government agencies at several levels publish information guides. Some publications deal with specific products or industries, while others are directories of sources of information. Some useful directories and other reports are published by groups not associated with any government, such as groups coordinated by Ralph Nader. For examples of specific books see the bibliography at the end of this chapter.

There are also several journals devoted to the consumer. The most widely known is *Consumer Reports,* a monthly magazine reporting on all sorts of products. This magazine lacks association with any company or governmental agency and contains tests and reports on consumer products. *Consumer Reports* also publishes an annual buyer's guide. Independent publications of this type provide useful, unbiased information on consumer goods. Smart consumers research before making major purchases such as a car, television or major appliance. Wise consumers also know that they can complain and that they have rights when products are defective. Using reference sources such as those discussed or listed in the bibliography helps the consumer in locating information when it is needed, e.g., names, addresses and phone numbers of corporations, governmental agencies or private groups that can answer questions or provide assistance.

In researching business or consumer information, periodicals and newspapers (Chapter 8) and government documents (Chapter 11) also provide information. The indexes to periodicals (*Business Periodicals Index*), the *Monthly Catalog* (for federal documents, especially the Consumer Protection Agency, see Chapter 11) and newspaper indexes (e.g., those of the *New York Times* and the *Wall Street Journal*) are also useful sources.

Exercises for Chapter 13

1. Find the names and addresses of firms manufacturing baseball bats.
2. Locate at least one industry study and one consumer organization study on the use of air bags in automobiles.
3. Locate and record the name, address and phone number of the consumer protection group nearest to your home.
4. Locate the corporate headquarters of General Foods and the name of the chief executive.

Important Books for Chapter 13

Ammer, Christine. *Dictionary of Business and Economics*, rev. ed. New York: Free Press, 1984.

Asch, Peter. *Consumer Safety Regulations: Putting a Price on Life and Limb*. New York: Oxford University Press, 1988.

Brobeck, Stephen. *The Product Safety Book: The Ultimate Consumer Guide to Products Hazards*. Edited by Jack for the Consumer Federation of America. New York: E. P. Dutton, 1983.

Brownstone, David M. *Where to Find Business Information: A Worldwide Guide for Everyone Who Needs the Answer to Business Questions*. 2nd ed. New York: John Wiley, 1982. Becoming dated but may still be useful.

Business Periodicals Index. New York: H. W. Wilson, 1958– , v. 1– (monthly). A cumulative subject index to periodicals in the field of accounting, advertising, banking and finance, general business insurance, labor and management, marketing and purchasing, public administration, taxation, specific businesses, industries and trades.

Consultants and Consulting Organizations Directory 1989: A Reference Guide to Concerns and Individuals, 9th ed. Detroit: Gale Research, 1989. 2 vols.

Consumer Reports, May 1936– . Mt. Vernon, NY: Consumer's Union of the United States, 1936– (monthly). *Buyer's Guide* is the December issue.

Consumer's Index to Product Evaluation and Information Sources. V. 1, no. 1– , Winter 1974– (quarterly with annual cumulations).

Daniells, Lorna M., et al. *How to Find Information About Companies*. 7th ed. Washington DC: Washington Researchers, 1989.

Directory of Government Agencies Safe-Guarding Consumer and Environment. Ed. 1, 1968– . Alexandria, VA: Serina Press, 1968– .

Elkington, John. *The Green Consumer: A Guide for the Environmentally Aware*. New York: Penguin, 1990.

Encyclopedia of Associations. 24th ed. Edited by Katherine Gruber. Detroit: Gale Research, 1989.

Encyclopedia of Business Information Sources. 7th ed. Edited by Paul Wasserman. Detroit: Gale Research, 1988. Supplement 1989.

Gillis, Jack. *The Used Car Book: An Easy-to-Use-Guide to Buying a Safe, Reliable, and Economical Used Car.* New York: Perenniel Library/ Harper & Row, 1988.

Horvitz, Simeon L. *Legal Protection for Today's Consumer.* 2nd ed. Dubuque, IA: Kendall/Hunt, 1989.

Middle Market Directory, 1964– . New York: Dun & Bradstreet, Inc., 1964– .

Million Dollar Directory, 1959– . New York: Dun & Bradstreet, Inc., 1959– (annual).

The New Palgrave: A Dictionary of Economics. New York: Stockton Press, 1987. 4 vols. This is the successor to the *Dictionary of Political Economy.*

Nisberg, Jay N. *Random House Handbook of Business Today.* New York: Random House, 1988.

Reader's Digest Consumer Advisor: An Action Guide to Your Rights. Edited by James A. Maxwell, rev. ed. Pleasantville, NY: Reader's Digest, 1989.

Salinger, Frank M. *A Guide to State Consumer Regulation.* New York: Executive Enterprises Publications, 1989. Part of the consumer credit handbook series.

Standard & Poor's Register of Corporations, Directors and Executives, United States and Canada, 1928– . New York, 1928– (annual).

Thomas' Register of American Manufacturers. New York: Thomas' Publishing, 190?– . (1990 edition has 23 volumes.)

U.S. Industrial Directory: The Direct Link to Industrial Products and Suppliers. Stamford, CT: Reed International/Cahners, 1990. 3 vols.

World Chamber of Commerce Directory. Loveland, OH: Worldwide Chamber of Commerce Directory, 1989– (annual).

14. Nonprint Materials and Special Services

Objectives

After studying this chapter the student shall be able to
- recognize the formats of microfilm and microfiche and explain how they may be used.
- use interlibrary loans to access remote materials
- use the OCLC system to locate materials
- request computer searches when needed

Nonprint Materials

Most libraries lump many things under the term *nonprint*. Often the term includes everything that is not a book or a periodical (that is, not printed on paper). The term then includes a variety of microprint formats, also records, audiotapes, videotapes, films and slides. Some libraries even lend the equipment needed for using these nonprint materials, such as microprint readers and cassette players.

The materials in microprint (reduced size) come in several formats. Microfilm is 16mm or 35mm and on reels. Microfiche is usually a 4×6 transparent card. The size of print on both microfilm and microform is usually reduced 24 times. Some microfiche is reduced 48 times. Ultrafiche is similar to microfiche, but the size of the cards may be 3×5 or 4×6 and the print is reduced 98 times. An ultrafiche (3×5)

141

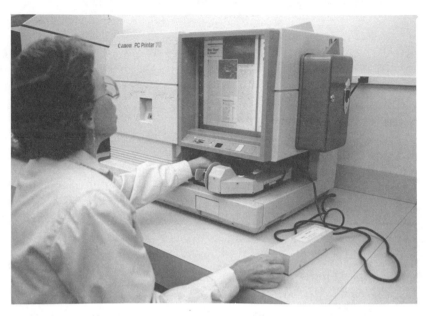

Working with microfilm is easy and comfortable. Some readers are also printers.

can contain up to 1,000 pages. Microcards can be 3×5, 4×6 or 5×8 in size but are opaque rather than transparent and may have printing on both sides of the card. Mechanical readers are needed to use all microforms. Some readers can be used with more than one format. Others are printers. They can be used to make "hard" or paper copy from the microform. The type of microform (negative or positive) and the type of copier will decide the format of the hard copy. Most microforms are positive, black letters on a white background. Some copiers use a dry photographic process so that the hard copy will be the opposite of what is seen on the screen. Positive film produces a negative image (white letters on a black background) hard copy. Some companies have designed reader/printers that are similar to photocopying machines and the hard copy is identical with what is seen on the screen. One brand of machine also senses if the microform is negative or positive and always produces a positive hard copy. These machines use plain paper which produces more permanent and readable copy.

Most readers have pictures or diagrams showing how to use the reader. If the directions are unclear or any doubt exists about the operation of the equipment, the user should request assistance from a member of the library staff. Improper use of equipment or the use of the wrong equipment can result in damage to the microform or the reader.

Special Library Services

Libraries provide services besides housing information. They provide reserve, reference and interlibrary loans. Reserves may range from holding a book that has been out in circulation to setting aside many books for a class. Reference services help users find the answers to questions. The help may vary from using the card catalog or OPAC to doing computer searches of databases. Most such searches available are of databases used to produce periodical indexes. These searches are generally faster and more complete than manual searches. Most libraries charge a fee for this type of service. One database in widespread use is PsycLIT (on-line and CD-ROM versions of *Psychological Abstracts*). From it one can obtain a computer generated list of summaries of all the journal articles on a particular topic. To obtain this information the searcher must provide key terms—descriptors—that are entered into the computer. The method is progressive in that the topic must be narrowed until the precise information can be processed. Usually librarians will provide professional help to do these searches, since it requires some experience to handle the terminal and to choose and enter appropriate descriptors. Some libraries have computer terminals available for student use. For more information, see chapters 9 and 15 on CD-ROM, databases and computers in libraries.

Interlibrary loan (ILL) is a procedure for borrowing books, periodicals and other materials from other libraries. It is extremely helpful in obtaining information not available locally. Each library has its own rules for interlibrary loans and it is probably necessary to ask at the reference or interlibrary loan librarian's desk for the forms and procedures to use. Some libraries charge for interlibrary loan service and others do not.

To speed up the processing of requests for ILL the student or faculty member should provide complete information. If for example a book is being requested, provide the author's complete name, the title of the book, publisher and date of publication. A request for a book by Jones, no first name or initial, even if the title, publisher and date are provided probably will be returned to the requester with a statement that there is insufficient information to process the request. If the needed material is a journal article, the requester must provide complete information: the full title of the journal with the volume number, date and pages, and the author's name and the title of the article. If the information is incomplete, the librarian is likely to return the request for additional information. Many librarians ask for a *verification*. The verification denotes where the user found the citation. Some libraries will not even begin to process on ILL request if the verification is not supplied. A valid verification would be any type of reference source discussed in this book.

If the request is for a book, the book will be sent. But, if the request is for a journal article, a photocopy will be sent. The time from presentation of the request to the ILL desk until the material arrives will be determined by the system(s) used by the borrowing library. For regional loans, local delivery systems are frequently used and the elapse time probably will be short. If the requested materials must come from a distant library, the lending library will be shipping the materials either by the U.S. Postal Service or United Parcel Service. Library materials shipped in either of these ways usually takes longer to arrive at the borrowing library. Students should plan.

OCLC

OCLC, the Online Computer Library Center, is an international on-line database of the holdings of more than 13,000 libraries. The OCLC headquarters and computers are located in Dublin, Ohio. The member libraries include the Library of Congress, the National Library of Medicine, the National Library of Canada and the British Lending Library. They provide cataloging information that is available then to all members. The system has more than 26 million records of all types of library materials: books, periodicals, pamphlets, records, audio tapes, video tapes, government documents, etc. OCLC numbers are assigned as new items are cataloged. The OCLC database may be searched in many ways: by author's name, title, author-title, series title, OCLC number, SuDoc number, ISBN number, ISSN number, LC card number and CODEN. ISBN is the international standard book number, and ISSN is the international standard serial number. CODEN is a code assigned to serials by indexing services such as *Biological Abstracts* and *Chemical Abstracts*.

The OCLC system provides member libraries with catalog cards and or magnetic tape of their holdings for use in the member library. Each record in the OCLC database has a holding's list attached to it. Thus every member library that has a copy of *War and Peace* will have its symbol attached to the record. If a library does not own a copy of *War and Peace* it can call up the record and see which libraries own a copy. Each edition, translation, etc., of *War and Peace* will have its own record and holding's list. Besides cataloging information and printing cards, the system simplifies transmitting interlibrary loan requests between member libraries. It also checks in periodicals, produces union lists of serials by regions or other specific areas and searches other databases from which periodical indexes are produced. Recently OCLC has added new services called EPIC and FirstSearch, reference services accessible via dedicated line OCLC terminals or via Internet. These services provide subject access to the OCLC on-line database and access to other databases. Some databases which are via EPIC and FirstSearch include Monthly Catalog, AIB/inform, Humanities Index (and other Wilson Indexes), MLA Bibliography and Dissertation Abstracts. As of February 1993, EPIC included 30 databases and First-Search 25 databases. Many are available on both systems. The holdings symbols for all libraries holding the item (book or periodical) are included in the display of each citation. Many databases available via OCLC are also accessible from DIALOG and other vendors. OCLC's charges are less than all other vendors. A library or individual can buy searches for FirstSearch at a fixed rate per search, there are no connect time or per item charges. EPIC and FirstSearch use different software so the user needs to learn two different sets of commands. FirstSearch is the easiest of all on-line systems and CD-ROM systems with the possible exception of InfoTrac's EasyTrac. OCLC charges for all services provided. Members of OCLC may participate in different components of the program.

Exercises for Chapter 14

1. Make a note of the ILL procedures and regulations in your library. Be sure to check on charges and the average length of time before requested materials arrive.
2. Ask the reference librarian if your library is a member of OCLC. If yes, ask about the scope of your library's participation in OCLC services.

Important Terms in Chapter 14

database	*nonprint*
OCLC	*microfiche*
Interlibrary Loan (ILL)	*microfilm*
ultrafiche	*verification*
microcards	*readers*

Important Books for Chapter 14

Boucher, Virginia. *Interlibrary Loan Practices Handbook.* Chicago: American Library Association, 1984.

Burwell, Helen P., and Carolyn N. Hills. *Directory of Fee-Based Information Services.* Houston, TX: Burwell Enterprises, 1984– (annual).

Guide to Microforms in Print. Westport, CT: Meckler, 1961– (annual). Author-title vol., subject volume and supplements.

Jackson, Mary E., ed. *Research Access Through New Technology.* New York: AMS Press, 1989.

Morris, Leslie R., and Sandra Chass Morris. *Interlibrary Loan Policies Directory.* 4th ed. New York: Neal-Schuman Publishers, 1991. Each entry lists policies, charges, address, phone numbers, FAX numbers, etc. for over 2,000 libraries. Directory is arranged by states.

Olle, James G. *A Guide to Sources of Information in Libraries.* Brookfield, VT: Gower Publishing, 1984.

Thompson, Sarah Katherine. *Interlibrary Loan Procedure Manual.* Chicago: Interlibrary Loan Committee, American Library Association, 1975.

15. On-Line Computer Use in Libraries and Schools

Objectives

After studying this chapter the student shall be able to
- identify where computers are used in the library
- identify available computer services in the library
- locate books and journals on computers
- recognize how databases are used

Definitions

Below are listed several terms commonly used in the discussion of computers.

Password—a secret word or symbol to be typed into a computer that allows the operator access to the system and prevents unauthorized access.

Program—instructions to the computer enabling the computer to perform desired tasks.

Hardware—the physical equipment: the computer, monitor, keyboard, etc.

Software—programs for the computer.

Keyboard—device for entering information into a computer by depressing keys. Computer keyboards are similar to typewriter keyboards.

Monitor—a screen for observing, viewing or controlling the operation of the computer. Most look very much like a TV screen. They may be colored or monochromatic (one color, usually green or amber).

Printer—a device that prints information from the computer; used to produce a "hard" (paper) copy of the desired data.

Floppy Disk (Diskette)—a flat circular plate with a magnetic surface, usually enclosed in a square paper envelope. Data (information) may be stored on one or both sides.

Modem—a device used to transmit computer signals over communication (usually telephone) facilities.

Peripherals—any device outside the central processing unit (disk drives, printers, monitors, etc.).

General Information

Within the next few years, most libraries will be using computers for a variety of tasks. Some libraries restrict the use of their computers to the library staff, while others allow public use. Those libraries having computers available for public use provide a wide range of assistance, including general instruction, instruction in programming and complex database searching. The kind and number of computer resources available and regulations regarding use vary from library to library. Most library computers available for use by the public are microcomputers (personal computers) with widespread familiarity and public availability, usually Apples, IBM PCs or compatibles, Commodores or TRS-80s.

Regulations on the use of microcomputers differ, as do the types of assistance available and the type of software owned by the library. Public libraries may allow a borrower to check out a computer and all the peripherals (disk drive, monitor, printer) needed to use the computer to its fullest, including software to be used with the computer. Usually, the equipment must be used in the library. Most libraries do not allow sign-up for more than a week in advance and restrict the number of hours per week an individual may use the equipment. Individuals may bring their software or use software belonging to the library. Arcade-type games are usually prohibited.

Often, users must prove their familiarity with computers before they are allowed to use them. Instructions in formal classes may be given or short orientations with the use of the equipment are required.

This permits most users to become familiar with the operation of the equipment. These restrictions apply to all users, children and adults. Public libraries usually choose at least some of their equipment to be compatible with equipment in the local school so that students will be able to complete school assignments in the public library after school hours.

The policy on charging for using computers in public libraries varies from library to library. Many libraries do not charge for equipment use, but will charge if the user damages software or equipment (just as if the user damaged a book, replacement costs are charged). Some libraries have installed coin operated computers at which the user gets several minutes for each coin. The school library or media center should be checked for availability of computers. The regulations for using computers differ from school to school, as they will from public library to public library.

Database searching is available in many libraries that have the equipment necessary to dial into the remote databases. Most libraries doing database searches use either BRS or DIALOG, two commercial vendors of computer services (see Chapter 9). To access these services, the library must have a microcomputer, a modem to dial long distance to the computer at the vendor and a password. Using services such as ONTYME, TYMENET or TELENET saves considerable money on the long distance telephone call. The vendors charge by the minute, so the more efficient the search is, the less it will cost. The librarian does a database search after discussion with the user about the specific information requested. Frequently the user and the librarian will conduct the search jointly. Using the microcomputer, the search can be stored in memory and printed out after the computer is disconnected from the database. This reduces cost, since many printers are slow and vendors charge by the minute of connect time (as does the telephone company). Some libraries will allow individuals to do database searches after they have had some instruction. Also, with the proper equipment and some cost, one can do database searching at home.

The catalog should be consulted for books on computers. For libraries using the Library of Congress system, books will be in the QA76s; in Dewey libraries, books will be in the 000s and the 510s. These are not the only locations, so the catalog should be checked. Libraries may have journals on computers and computing. The periodical's list contains the items the library subscribes to that deal with computers. Other popular computer magazines are *Family Computing*,

Creative Computing, Byte and Computer World. Some journals are devoted to specific computers: Apples, Commodores, Radio Shack (TRS), IBM PC, etc.

Exercises for Chapter 15

1. Determine if your library has computers. If so, what kind?
2. Who is allowed to use the equipment?
3. List the rules for software use in your library.
4. List the rules for using the computers in your library.
5. To what computer periodicals does your library subscribe?
6. If your school doesn't have any computers in the library, check the public library and see what it has.

Important Terms in Chapter 15

database	*hardware*
software	*microcomputer*
vendor	*peripherals*
terminal	*printer*
monitor	*floppy disk (diskette)*
modem	*keyboard*
password	

Important Books for Chapter 15

Alberico, Ralph. *Microcomputers for the Online Searcher: Media and Tools for Value-Added Online Searching Small Computers in Libraries*. Westport, CT: Meckler Corp., 1987.

Connors, Martin. *Online Database Search Services Directory*, 2nd ed. Detroit: Gale Research, 1988.

Daniel, Evelyn H. *Media and Microcomputers in the Library: A Selected Annotated Resource Guide*. Phoenix, AZ: Oryx, 1984.

Directory of Online Databases. Santa Monica, CA: Cuadra Associates, 1979– . Volume 1– , Fall 1979– .

Directory of Periodicals Online, 1st ed. 1985– . Washington, DC: Federal Document Retrieval, Inc., 1985– . Published in 3 vols. Volume 1—News, law and business. Volume 2—Medicine and social sciences. Volume 3—Science and technology.

Edelhart, Mike. *Omni Online Directory,* revised ed. New York: Collier Brooks/Macmillan, 1985.

Fenichel, Carol H., and Thomas H. Hogan. *Online Searching: A Primer,* 3rd ed. Medford, NJ: Learned Info., 1989.

Guide to Online Databases. Boca Raton, FL: Newsletter Management, 1983.

Hall, James L. *Online Bibliographic Databases: An International Directory,* 4th ed. London: Aslib, 1986. Distributed by Gale Research.

Hoover, Ryan E., ed. *Online Search Strategies.* White Plains, NY: Knowledge Industry, 1982.

Jensen, Patricia E. *Using OCLC: A How-to-Do-It Manual for Librarians.* New York: Neal-Schuman, 1989. How to do it series no. 5.

Kesselman, Martin, and Sarah Watstein. *End-User Searching: Services and Providers.* Chicago: American Library Association, 1988.

Software Review, v. 1– . Westport, CT: Meckler, 1982– .

Thacker, Kathleen, ed. *Directory of Computerized Data Files.* Springfield, VA: National Technical Information, U.S. Department of Commerce, 1989.

Thompson, James. *The End of Libraries.* Clive Bingley, 1982; distributed by Shoe String Press.

16. Hints for Writing Papers

Objectives

After studying this chapter the student shall be able to
- use note cards as an adjunct to library research
- use a database to take notes
- label cards for retrieval and bibliography writing
- be aware of the various uses of word processors in footnoting, outlining, indexing and composing papers
- find an appropriate method for citing other authors
- distinguish between primary and secondary sources and know the advantages of using primary sources
- define and avoid plagiarism
- understand copyright and the rules governing the photocopying of material

General Information

Writing term papers and reports can be a laborious process, particularly if the writer does not use efficient methods of data collection and retrieval. Thus, it is important to develop techniques that will enable one to avoid unnecessary work. The following discussion is not meant as a comprehensive discourse on how to write term papers since there are many excellent term paper manuals that may be consulted for this purpose. Rather, hints that the authors have found useful in writing papers are presented.

Taking Notes with Note Cards

The first step to writing the paper is to conceptualize the topic. Research in the library follows. How to find materials has been discussed extensively in the prior chapters. Gathering and transcribing data in a useful form so that it may be retrieved later must be done efficiently. One extremely useful way to saving data is by using lined index cards. Each piece of data should be abstracted and transcribed to cards, preferably the 4×6 or the 5×8 cards. This may sound simple minded and one may ask why notebook paper is not equally good. Using cards has several advantages. First, a card or set of cards can be easily sorted by topics later and then resorted using other categories; this is more difficult with notebook paper. Second, more materials on the same topic or from the same source may be added more easily later by just adding cards. Third, when writing an outline cards may be sorted by subheadings.

For writing note cards, the following hints will be helpful. Include on the first card for each source the information that will be needed in the footnote and the bibliography. On each subsequent card for the source show the author and the date of the work at the top. This will save all the accumulated work that has already been done in case the cards get dropped or mixed up. Frequently when doing research reviews, one may find several articles by the same author written at different times. When the paper is written it is difficult to recall from which articles that piece of information derives, thus the need for the author and date on each card.

Taking Notes with a Database

Using a database for note taking can be an invaluable aid to the student. Databases allow information to be stored in records and fields. Each record contains all the information about a particular source, magazine article, book or reference citation. Within each record, many fields may be designated to contain selected information about that record. Thus, for each source, there is a record with multiple fields.

As the student finds additional articles, he can enter the information about the article into the database by record. A typical record might look like the following:

Record #1

Field Name

Author	Mills, Frederick A.
Title	"Databasing for Fun and Profit"
Journal	*Popular Databasing*
Date	July 1985
Volume #	7:12
Pages	35–43
Content	This article contains information about the newest databases available; with emphasis on their application at home.
Subject	Databases

Other fields may be added as needed. The better databases allow 20 or more fields for each record. Once the information has been entered (this can be done a little at a time) it can be selected in a variety of ways for later use by sorting by any of the fields. Sorting the above record by author will give the bibliographic references necessary for the report.

Another sort by subject provides clusters of records that form sections of chapters to be written. Another sorting by date would be helpful in writing in a time or historic framework. Instead of carrying around many individual index cards, the student can store all the information necessary for writing the paper on a single diskette.

The fields and records may be output to a printer in any way the user desires. For example, a printed list with just the authors' names, or just the names of the journal articles, could be printed out. Furthermore, the format is flexible so that the spacing and line setups can be determined by the author. As more entries are added to the database the information is automatically added, and revised copies of the lists can be printed out in a matter of minutes. This feature alone could save hours of sorting and typing.

The writer must learn to use the database. But this time is well spent. No special knowledge of the computer is necessary to begin working with a database. Anyone can sit at the computer, follow the instruction manual and begin databasing in a matter of minutes. More involved uses of the program will become evident as the student uses a program more. Usually, students may obtain databases from school or purchase them at minimal cost.

Word Processing

Students should use word processors to construct papers and theses. These are readily available for loan or may be purchased inexpensively. Writing a paper using a word processor takes most of the drudgery out of the process. It allows for instant corrections as you are typing. This takes the fear out of the process and greatly increases one's typing speed and confidence at the keyboard. Editing can be done directly on the keyboard or from a hard (printed) copy of the text. Words can be changed, sentences moved, paragraphs may be added or deleted instantaneously and the revised version can be printed out immediately. Large amounts of text can be stored on floppy disks rather than on reams of paper and large numbers of index cards. Many word processing packages provide a spelling checker integrated into the software package which will automatically check the spelling of all words in the text. Some programs even offer substitute words to use. Most word processors also include a thesaurus that provides synonyms. One merely points to a word in the text, hits a key and a list of substitutes appear.

Also one may use a word processor for other purposes besides composing documents. Footnoting is easy using a word processing program such as WordPerfect. The program allows footnotes to cross-reference documents in many ways. The reader can be informed to seek additional information on other pages, in other chapters, in other paragraphs and in end notes. An automatic reference numbering system allows the writer to renumber his footnotes automatically as new ones are added or deleted.

As one is writing, key words or phrases may be marked for later use in a table of contents or for indexes at the back of the book. Word-Perfect has a feature for outlining that automatically creates the necessary levels using Roman numerals, letters and many subdivisions. Paragraphs may be numbered for future editing, graphics may be inserted into text and calculations may be done without leaving the program. As with the databases, some time must be spent learning to use a word processor, but again the time will be well spent. The reason for this will become apparent when one writes just one paper on the word processor.

Footnoting

Deciding what must be footnoted or cited is a difficult decision. Authors are entitled to credit for their work, just as the student wants a grade or credit for the paper he or she has written. It is unfair, immoral and may be illegal to use information written by another author without giving the appropriate credit to the author. Some information is common knowledge and does not have to be cited. For example, the name of the 13th president of the United States, dates of important events and other data are so widely known that authors need not give credit. This kind of information, though one has to look it up, need not be cited. Still, specific information, such as an author's written opinion and other unique productions such as research findings should always be cited. One should never copy from another work unless it is made clear that the material is a quotation and the author is cited.

When reusing information from another source, it is still necessary to cite the author even if the words that are used by the student are different. If the idea was found in someone else's work, it must be cited. It is not only ethically and morally an imperative, but copying without citation could result in dire consequences to the student. All colleges have severe rules against copying or, as it is called, plagiarism. Students have been expelled or given a failing grade because their papers had been shown to contain material that was plagiarized. A college handbook is a good source of information on the college's policy on plagiarism.

Copying from a source without credit is analogous to stealing. But one can avoid the problem. Whenever there is the slightest doubt as to whether one should cite something, cite it. It is preferable to cite too much than to omit a citation that is necessary.

One simple and widely used method of notation consists of inserting parenthetically the author's last name, a comma and the date directly in the text as needed. For example, a recent study has shown that boys and girls do not significantly differ in total reading ability at the 8th grade level (Wolf, 1978).

This seems a logical way to cite works by other authors. However, instructors may insist on a particular format for citations and bibliographic listings, and the student should make sure that they use the required format. If the instructor lacks preference, the student could well use the method described above for citations and the bibliographic style that is found after each chapter in this text. Anyhow, one must get the information correctly transcribed the first time, since it may be extremely difficult to find it later. Transcribe the bibliographic information plus the citation onto the first card exactly as it should appear in the final paper. This will make it easier when the paper is written. Use as many cards as necessary for that source, putting the citation on each card. For example, "(Wolf, 1975)." A numbering system also will be useful with multiple cards.

Primary Sources

To develop precision in researching a topic the student should use as many primary resources as possible. Primary sources are those that are written or reported by the author. Secondary sources, on the other hand, are reports, abstracts or descriptions based on the primary sources or taken from the primary source. Primary sources may often be more accurate than secondary sources, particularly where the secondary source extensively summarizes the original material. Secondary source writers may misquote, misinterpret or distort the original materials. This usually occurs in reviews of the literature in a particular field. For example, in the *Annual Review of Psychology* the reviewer must abstract one dozen research articles on a topic such as psychotherapy. Often in condensing the findings, gross errors occur as well as subtle differences in meaning.

Researchers should find out whether the information being obtained derives from a primary or secondary source. Detective work should reveal original sources that provide more accurate data. These should be consulted when possible.

Copyright

Copyright is a means of protecting the rights of authors, composers and artists. Copyright laws protect original works from being copied, except for specific conditions outlined in the law, and insure that the individual creating the copyrighted materials receives payment (royalties) for the sale of his or her works. The copyright law is specific in detailing requirement for receiving a copyright (the copyright office is a part of the Library of Congress), and in the placement of the copyright statement in published materials. To locate copyright

Using the copying machine.

information in published materials, look on the title page or the back of the title page for the date. The law is also specific about the conditions for reproducing copyrighted materials and the penalty for violating the law. The law provides stiff penalties for infringement on the rights of the copyright owners (author or publisher) when copies are made without the written permission of the copyright owner. Today's high quality, rapid photocopying machines provide the means of violating the law, and students and faculty should not make multiple copies of protected materials without permission. A single copy of a page or two of a journal article or a book, to be used for scholarly purposes, is usually permissible. Yet, credit should be given to the author and permission obtained from the copyright owner. This may be obtained by writing the publisher. Under no conditions should multiple copies be made without the permission of the publisher.

Term Paper Guides (see also Chapter 5)

Campbell, William Giles, et al. *Form and Style: Theses, Reports, Term Papers*, 8th ed. Houghton, 1990.

Fleischer, Eugene R. *A Style Manual for Citing Microform and Non-print Media.* Chicago: American Library Association, 1978.

Lunsford, Andrea, and Robert Connors. *The St. Martin's Handbook.* New York: St. Martin's Press, 1989. (This volume contains several style sheets including the American Psychological Association and the Modern Language Association.)

MLA Handbook for Writers of Research Papers, 3rd ed. Edited by Joseph Gibaldi and Walter S. Achtert. New York: Modern Language Association, 1988.

Taylor, Gordon. *The Student's Writing Guide for the Arts and Social Sciences.* New York: Cambridge University Press, 1989.

Turabian, Kate L. *A Manual for Writers of Term Papers, Theses, and Dissertations*, 5th ed. Chicago: University of Chicago Press, 1986.

Appendix: Answers to Exercises

Chapter 1

Each library will differ in layout and regulations.

Chapter 2

1. Snow (LCSH 1992 v. 4, p. 4255)
   (May Subd Geog) [GB2401–GB2597 (Physical Geography)] [QC929.
   S7 (Meterology)]
   BT   Precipitation (Meteorology)
   .
   .

   Weather
   NT   Avalanches
       .
       .

       Wind-snow interaction
   —   Electric Properties
   —   Measurement
       BT Snow Surveys
   —   Removal
       USE Snow Removal
   —   Surveying
       USE Snow Surveys
   —   Thermal Properties

2. (A) Q 121 M3 1987
   (B) PE 1625 O87 1989
   (C) AY 67 N5 W7
   (D) JK 516 C57
   (E) AG 5 K 315

3. First line is title (b), second author (a), third subject (c)

4. (A) 520
   (B) 599.9
   (C) 599.8
   (D) 000

5. (A) E–F
   (B) L
   (C) ND
   (D) NE
   (E) R
   (F) G

6. (A) 1979
   (B) Princeton, N.J.
   (C) ND699.K3W43
   (D) Peg Weiss
   (E) $30.00
   (F) 2
   (G) Kandinsky in Munich
   (H) yes
   (I) 759.7
   (J) Princeton University Press

Chapter 3

If you have access to an OPAC try these. The results will vary depending on the library's holdings. If your library does not have any books by
Jean M. Auel, choose another author. Be sure to try question 4 even
if your library has no books by Jean M. Auel.

Chapter 4

1. Last Supper (LCSH 1992 v. 3, pp. 2561–2566)
   [BT 420] Here are entered works on the final meal of Christ with his
   apostles...
   UF   Jesus Christ—Last Supper
   BT   Dinners and dining in the Bible
   RT   Lord's Supper
        Maundy Thursday
        Passover in the New Testament
   Last Supper (Mural painting)
   Last Supper in Art

2. Some examples are:
   Jewish-Arab Relations (LCSH 1992 v. 2, p. 2379)
   Israel-Arab Conflicts (LCSH 1992 v. 2, p. 2332)
   Israel-Arab Border Conflicts, 1949– (LCSH 1992 v. 2, p. 2332)
   Palestinian Arabs (LCSH 1992 v. 3, p. 3358)

3. Some examples are:
   (A) Southern States—History—War of 1812
   (B) Reinsurance (may subd geo)
   (C–E) See answers to question 1 above.

4. Answers will vary depending on the topic chosen.

Chapter 5

1. (A) Faulkner, William (1, 2, 4 will vary from library to library) 3.
       Examples: Bassett, John Earl. *William Faulkner, An Annotated
       Checklist of Criticism,* and McHaney, Thomas L. *William
       Faulkner: A Reference Guide.*
2. (A) BIP 1992–1993   68 entries
   (B) CBI 1990 v. 1, p. 2106   10 entries
   (C) Political Science, Biography, Great Britain are some examples
   (D) LC-Books Subj. 1970–74, v. 17, pp. 32–34

Chapter 6

1. Have you looked at this book carefully?
2. For example—Gilbert, Martin. *Winston Churchill,* v. 8, *"Never Despair,"* 1945–1965. See *Book Review Digest* 1989, p. 603 (4 reviews listed.)

Chapter 7

Questions 1–10, 13–14 involve the varying resources of individual libraries. For 10 (C), see any of the comparative guides like those published by Barrons or Peterson.

11. (A) Zip codes, for large cities a city street map and places of interest, instructions for using the yellow pages, large ads in addition to listings.
    (B) Yes, usually one of the first of the yellow paes.
    (C) Yes, usually one of the first few white pages.
    (D) Types of business and industry, schools (special, private, public), professionals (lawyers, doctors, dentists).

12. (A) McGraw-Hill Book Co., 1221 Ave. of the Americas, New York, N.Y. 10021. (212) 512-2000.
    (B) Population as of 1990 was 467,610
    (C) Population as of 1990 was 81,140,922, area 756,198 sq. miles, President Carlos Salinas de Gortari (Dec. 1988)

Chapter 8

Questions 1–3, 7 will vary from library, and student to student.

4. v. 50, 1990 p. 983
   v. 44, p. 950
   v. 39, p. 713
   v. 34, p. 563

5. 1990, v. 50, pp. 993–994, 14 see also headings, 11 major subheadings, one of these has 7 subheadings. 1974–75, v. 34, p. 566, 3 see also headings and 2 subheadings.

6. *Education Index* 1991–1992, p. 672
   Social Sciences Index 1991–1992, p. 974
   Business Periodicals Index 1991–1992, pp. 1924–1925

Chapter 9

Answers will vary from library to library.

Chapter 10

1. Answers will vary from library to library. See the bibliography at the end of Chapter 10.

2. (A) For locations see *Granger's Index,* 7th ed., p. 838.
   (B) See entries in *Short Story Index* under Clemens, Samuel Langhorne and under Twain, Mark. Some stories are: *The Man Who Corrupted Hadleyburg, The California Tale, The Celebrated Jumping Frog of Calaveras County* (also known as *The Notorious Jumping Frog of Calaveras County*), *The Invalid's Story, Three Thousand Years Among the Microbes, Dick Baker's Cat, Jim Baker's Bluejay Yarn,* and *Jim Blaine and His Grandfather's Ram.*
   (C) Hint. Check BIP, etc. for publishing date. See *Book Review Index* 1965–84 Cumulation, v. 2, p. 973.
   (D) For example see *Reader's Guide* under Motion Picture Reviews, v. 50, 1990, p. 1261.
   (E) Some of the plays by Simon are: *California Suite, God's Favorite, The Good Doctor, The Odd Couple, The Prisoner of Second Avenue, The Sunshine Boys, Visitor from Forest Hills, Barefoot in the Park, Come Blow Your Hour, The Gingerbread Boy, The Last of the Red Hot Lovers, Plaza Suite, Brighton Beach Memoirs, Broadway Bound,* and *Biloxi Blues.* For reviews see: RGPL under Simon, Neil or see *New York Times Index* under Theater (see 1988, p. 1271 for reviews of *Biloxi Blues* and *Broadway Bound*).
   (F) For example see *Essay and General Literature Index,* v. 8, p. 270–271, Clemens, Samuel Langhorne, or v. 10 under Twain, Mark, pp. 1672–1675.

Chapter 11

1. For some examples see the bibliography at the end of Chapter 11.

2. (B) Iran-Contra Affair, 1985– . See the subject index to the *Monthly Catalog*, 1989, pp. I–1555 to I–1556.

3. Check any of the following: *Congressional Directory, Congressional Staff Directory, Almanac of American Politics, Taylor's Encyclopedia,* the Blue Book for your state.

4. (A) Alben W. Barkley. (Examples of sources—any volume of *Taylor's Encyclopedia,* any encyclopedia.
   (B) Use the *U.S. Government Manual* or check any encyclopedia.
   (C) Check the latest volume of *Taylor's Encyclopedia.*

5. Answers will vary.

Chapter 12

1. For examples of titles see bibliography in Chapter 12.

2. (A and B) Will vary from student to student.
   (C–E) Check such sources as *Biography Index, Personal Name Index to the New York Times Index, Biography and Genealogy Master Index.*
   (C) *Biography and Genealogy Master Index* 1981–85, Cumulation, v. 1, p. 788.
   (D) *Biography Index,* v. 10, p. 623.

3. Check the back of *Biography Index* by occupation, v. 7, p. 846 for example.

Chapter 13

1. See *Thomas' Register,* v. 1, p. 1356, 1990.

2. For examples see *Business Periodicals Index,* Air Bag Restraint Systems see Automobiles—Air Bags. 1991–1992, p. 306.

3. See a directory such as *Encyclopedia of Associations.*

4. See directories such as *Moody's Industrial Manual, Million Dollar Directory.* See index in *Moody's,* blue pages and note that 1990 ed. says see under Philip Morris companies, pp. 3297–3314.

Chapters 14 and 15

Answers will vary from library to library.

Index